34320000079300

D0509347

SHARPENING BASICS

Patrick Spielman

 Sterling Publishing Co., Inc.   New York

INCHES TO CENTIMETERS

INCHES	CM	INCHES	CM	INCHES	CM	INCHES	CM
1/8	0.3	9	22.9	24	61.0	39	99.1
1/4	0.6	10	25.4	25	63.5	40	101.6
3/8	1.0	11	27.9	26	66.0	41	104.1
1/2	1.3	12	30.5	27	68.6	42	106.7
5/8	1.6	13	33.0	28	71.1	43	109.2
3/4	1.9	14	35.6	29	73.7	44	111.8
7/8	2.2	15	38.1	30	76.2	45	114.3
1	2.5	16	40.6	31	78.7	46	116.8
2	5.1	17	43.2	32	81.3	47	119.4
3	7.6	18	45.7	33	83.8	48	121.9
4	10.2	19	48.3	34	86.4	49	124.5
5	12.7	20	50.8	35	88.9	50	127.0
6	15.2	21	53.3	36	91.4		
7	17.8	22	55.9	37	94.0		
8	20.3	23	58.4	38	96.5		

Basics Series

Band Saw Basics

Cabinetry Basics

Radial Arm Saw Basics

Router Basics

Scroll Saw Basics

Sharpening Basics

Table Saw Basics

Other Books by Patrick Spielman

Alphabets and Designs for Wood Signs

(and Sherry Spielman)

Carving Large Birds

(and Bill Dehos)

Carving Wild Animals: Life-Size Wood Figures

(and Bill Dehos)

Classic Fretwork Scroll Saw Patterns

(and James Reidle)

Gluing and Clamping

Making Country-Rustic Wood Projects

(and Sherry Spielman Valitchka)

Making Wood Decoys

Making Wood Signs

Realistic Decoys

(and Keith Bridenhagen)

Router Basics

Router Handbook

Router Jigs & Techniques

Scroll Saw Basics

Scroll Saw Country Patterns

(and Sherry Spielman Valitchka)

Scroll Saw Handbook

Scroll Saw Fretwork Patterns

(and James Reidle)

Scroll Saw Fretwork Techniques and Projects

(and James Reidle)

Scroll Saw Pattern Book

(and Patricia Spielman)

Scroll Saw Puzzle Patterns

(and Patricia Spielman)

Spielman's Original Scroll Saw Patterns

(and Patricia Spielman)

Victorian Scroll Saw Patterns

Working Green Wood with PEG

Library of Congress Cataloging-in-Publication Data

Spielman, Patrick E.
　　Sharpening basics / Patrick Spielman.
　　　　p.　　cm.
　　Includes index.
　　ISBN 0-8069-7226-2
　　1. Sharpening of tools.　2. Wood-cutting tools.　I. Title
TJ1280.S647　1991
621.9′2—dc20
　　　　　　　　　　　　　　91-19984
　　　　　　　　　　　　　　CIP

Copyright © 1991 by Patrick Spielman
Published by Sterling Publishing Company, Inc.
387 Park Avenue South, New York, N.Y. 10016
Distributed in Canada by Sterling Publishing
% Canada Manda Group, P.O. Box 920, Station U
Toronto, Ontario, Canada M8Z 5P9
Distributed in Great Britain and Europe by Cassell PLC
Villiers House, 41/47 Strand, London WC2N 5JE, England
Distributed in Australia by Capricorn Link Ltd.
P.O. Box 665, Lane Cove, NSW 2066
Manufactured in the United States of America
All rights reserved
Sterling ISBN 0-8069-7226-2

Contents

ACKNOWLEDGMENTS

Many individuals and various companies have assisted in this work, and a sincere thank-you is expressed to all, and especially to the following: Glen Davidson of Welliver and Sons, for allowing material to be used from his fine book, *Tool Grinding and Sharpening Handbook*; Zach Etheridge of Highland Hardware, Atlanta, Georgia for his generous efforts and technical expertise; Rob Russell of the Russellworks, for his original tips and good sources; Doug Pinkham of Makita U.S.A.; Bob McGee of Eze-Lap Diamond Products; Leonard G. Lee, President, Lee Valley Tools Ltd.; Robert Varzino, Sears Power Tool Division; Gene Sliga, Delta International Machinery Corp.; Peter Segal, Garrett Wade Co., Inc.; David Draves, Woodcraft Supply Corp.; Ron Hock, Hock's Knives; Renee T. LaRocca, Dremel Power Tools; Fred Damsen, Woodline; Roger Becker, President, Martek International, Inc.; artists Sherri Spielman Valitchka, James Rericha, and Ralph Murre; and typist Julie Kiehnau.

INTRODUCTION

It is essential that all woodworkers learn how to sharpen their tools. Dull tools are dangerous to use, and usually do not cut well. A properly sharpened tool will not only cut cleanly, it will cause few accidents because it is easier to control. It also requires less physical and machine power, and, therefore, reduces wear in motors and fatigue in humans.

All tools will eventually have to be sharpened. In fact, some brand-new tools such as certain plane irons and carving tools are sold with the understanding that the customer must do the final sharpening, before the tools can be used. And, more and more often I'm finding that new tools expected to be sharp in fact need immediate additional sharpening to perform satisfactorily.

Though there are professional sharpening services available, the home woodworker will find it less costly and more practical to sharpen his tools himself. In fact, because of the costs and time factors associated with professional sharpening services, some of the tools made today, such as power-driven bits and knives, are disposable.

In its simplest context, sharpening is the wearing away of one material (a cutting tool) with another material that's harder. It is essentially an abrasive cutting process much like that of sanding wood. (See Illus. i-1.) In fact, some of the same abrasives and tools used to smooth wood are also used to sharpen many woodworking tools.

To beginners, tool sharpening may appear to be a complicated and confusing skill to learn. One reason is that because any one tool can be sharpened in a variety of ways, expert woodworkers have different approaches to sharpening. These approaches may be technically sound and effective, but few are in complete agreement.

To add to the confusion, many sharpening aids have recently flooded the market. Many are effective; others aren't. These new products, along with the new abrasive sharpening mediums that include Japanese waterstones, ceramics, and diamond sharpeners, threaten to replace the conventional systems.

But sharpening can be a skill that is easily learned. The key is to acquire the essential infor-

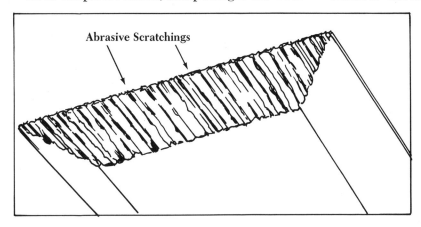

Abrasive Scratchings

Illus. i-1. *This enlarged simulation of a chisel's bevelled surface shows the microscopic scoring and furrowing produced by the sharpening abrasive.*

mation needed to determine if a tool is sharp, and, if it is not, how much and the best ways to sharpen it.

What is a sharp tool? Basically, a sharp tool is one that can cut effectively. This does not necessarily mean that the tool has to be sharpened to its optimum cutting angle. Many tools can still cut effectively even if they have not been sharpened to their precise cutting angles. The following list contains descriptions of the various conditions a cutting edge may be in:

1. **Destroyed or ruined.** Beyond any possible repair.

2. **Worn out.** Used up; no longer sharpenable.

3. **Damaged, or abused.** An edge that needs major reworking. (See Illus. i-2 and i-3.)

Illus. i-2. *The chipped edges of this carbide-tipped bit will require professional grinding so that they will be restored and the tool will be balanced. Such situations reduce the overall service life of the tool because so much material must be removed.*

Illus. i-3. *A severely damaged tool caused by inattentive grinding. This jointer knife was overheated and burned, which softened the composition of the metal at the edge. All of the material above the dotted line must be reground to restore a new bevel with a serviceable edge. (A bevel is the inclined surface that is sharpened on the tool.)*

4. **Dull.** Sharpenable. (See Illus. i-4.)

5. **Dirty.** (Pitch-loaded, rusty, etc.) Can be cleaned.

6. **Half sharp.** Needs minor touch-up.

7. **Sharp.** Serviceable for the task at hand. (See Illus. i-5.)

8. **Super Sharp.** Sometimes desirable for certain tools and the highest personal standards.

Not all tools need a major grinding or removal of metal. Many times a tool only needs to be cleaned of rust, pitch, or resin build-up to perform much better. But, even if the cutting edge is very dull or even abused, it can be reworked into a useful, sharp one.

It's not always practical to make some tools "super-sharp." A carpenter's or plumber's wood chisel generally does not have to be as sharp as that of an instrument maker or wood carver.

Wood materials do not cut alike. As a general rule, softwoods require much keener edges than

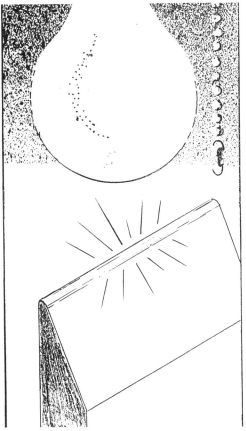

do hardwoods. Hardwoods can often be cut with a comparatively dull tool, but this is a dangerous process that will require a much more concentrated effort. The same dull edge that can cut hardwood will tear apart softwood. (See Illus. i-6 and i-7.) Remember, too, that man-made material such as plywood and particleboard will dull tools more quickly than solid wood.

Many beginners believe that a tool that is made of harder metal can be given a sharper and longer-lasting cutting edge than one made of softer metal. This is not accurate. A case in point is carbide. Carbide is one of the hardest of the man-made materials. It is also one of the most brittle. (See Illus. i-2.) That is why power-driven carbide tools are ground to comparatively blunt or more obtuse angles. (See Illus. i-9.) Carbide is too brittle to be used on hand-carving tools, which require cutting edges with very acute angles. Carbide would chip or fracture too easily. It will, however, remain moderately sharp much longer than steel tools used under the same conditions. That is why carbide tools are good for

Illus. i-4. *A visual inspection shows light reflecting from a dull edge.*

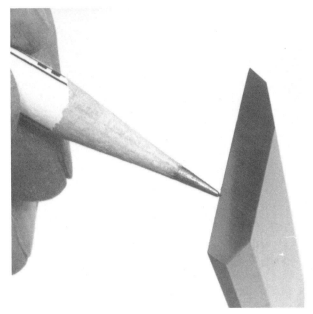

Illus. i-5. *The cutting edge of this sharp chisel does not reflect any light.*

Illus. i-6. *Two cross-grain cuts made in hard oak with woodcarver's parting tools. The cut on the left was made with a sharp tool. The cut on the right was made with a fairly dull tool, but with considerably more effort.*

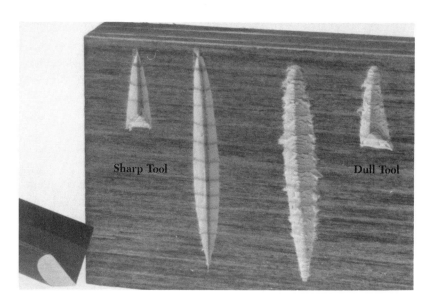

Illus. i-7. *Cuts in soft pine made with the same two tools used to cut the oak board in Illus. i-6. The short and long cuts at the left were made with a sharp parting tool. The two cuts at the right were made with the dull tool. Note the torn fibres and overall roughness of the cuts resulting from using the dull tool.*

Illus. i-8. *An end view of a carbide-tipped router bit. Note the fairly blunt angles ground in the bit.*

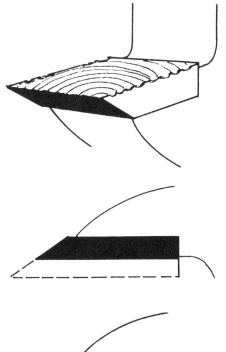

cutting plywood, particleboard, and hard plastic laminate. However, it is not advisable, or even possible, to give carbide a super-sharp edge, as can be done to steel tools. The best cutting hand tools are made of metals that are relatively hard, yet can take a very keen edge.

Regardless of how adept a woodworker becomes at sharpening, he should still occasionally use a professional sharpening service. Some of the more sophisticated wood-cutting tools such

Illus. i-9. *Examples of unacceptable grinding by a sharpening service. Above: This rough, scored finish that resulted from using too coarse an abrasive reduces edge life and sharpness. Center: Excessive material removal shortens useful tool life. Below: Uneven grinding changes the cutting angle (tool geometry), which has a negative impact on the cutting efficiency of the tool.*

as spiral cutters and carbide-tipped blades should be ground and balanced by professionals. Even some of the power-driven cutters that you will learn to sharpen and touch up yourself should be intermittently sharpened professionally, to ensure that safe rotational balance and proper cutting angles are maintained.

Inattentive or careless sharpening can downgrade a tool very quickly, and even severely damage or ruin it. Illus. i-3 and i-6 show visible examples of work not acceptable, especially if done by a sharpening service. Non-visible conditions of poor grinding by a sharpening service may not show up until the tool is used. If a tool has micro-chips on its carbide-tipped edge or if its edge dulls prematurely, this suggests that the tool was excessively heated during grinding. A good grinding service would use wet grinding equipment and put a fine, smooth finish on the ground surface.

The following chapters give an overview of popular sharpening devices and the basic techniques for sharpening many popular homeshop woodworking tools. Although step-by-step methods for sharpening every conceivable tool are not given, you will learn by applying these principles that you can sharpen a broad range of different tools. Plane irons, and wood chisels, for example, are essentially sharpened the same way as are other single-bevel hand tools such as spokeshaves and drawknives.

Please note the Glossary that appears on pages 126 and 127. This Glossary clarifies the terms that appear in the chapters. It will help simplify the sharpening process and should be referred to as you read the information presented in the following pages.

Patrick Spielman

Chapter 1

BENCH SHARPENING TOOLS AND ACCESSORIES

This chapter explores popular non-powered tools and accessories used in tool sharpening. No attempt is made to rate any item in importance or value because needs vary individually.

Bench "Stones"

One of the major items a tool-sharpening craftsman needs is a bench stone. The word stone is a misnomer is some instances because products of other than natural stone origin are now used in the manufacture of stones. Although natural sharpening stones are still available, bonded man-made abrasives grains, ceramics, and microscopic diamond crystals bonded to steel plates comprise today's sharpening "stones." These types of stones are described below.

Coated Abrasives

Coated abrasives (sandpapers) are inexpensive and convenient, and are perhaps one of the most underutilized tool sharpening mediums. (See Illus. 1-1 and 1-2.) Man-made aluminum oxide (emery) and silicon-carbide abrasive grains used to make modern "sandpapers" are essentially the

very same materials bonded together to make block bench sharpening stones, hones, slips, and grinding wheels. (See Illus. 1-3.)

Illus. 1-1. *Sheet abrasives suitable for economical tool sharpening include cloth-backed emery (aluminum oxide) and cloth- and paper-backed silicon-carbide abrasives. Note: Cut strips, when taped to one end of a piece of plywood, make a good stone substitute or "slick."*

sive particles are hard and, when backed with paper or cloth, can handle many sharpening jobs.

Silicon-carbide crystals are blue-black in color and considerably harder and sharper than aluminum oxide. Because it is hard, a silicon-carbide crystal fractures, constantly breaking and exposing new, sharp cutting points. Wet-dry paper-backed silicon-carbide abrasives can be used with oil or water as lubricants to cool and clean the cutting action. Aluminum-oxide and silicon-carbide sheet abrasives are available in coarse to fine grits (600), and will sharpen most home-shop cutting tools except tungsten carbide tools.

Oilstones

Oilstones have been around well over 100 years. Thin oil is a sharpening lubricant and cleaner when oilstones are used.

Oilstones are either man-made (like coated abrasives) or are quarried from natural stones. Most oilstones fall into three distinct categories: (1) natural or Arkansas, (2) aluminum oxide (called "India" by the Norton Company), and (3) silicon carbide (called "Crystolon" by the Norton Company).

Illus. 1-2. *A piece of fine-grit emery cloth or silicon-carbide abrasive that is held tautly around a dowel makes a very good round slipstone.*

Aluminum oxide can be of various colors. Emery is simply a dark variation of aluminum oxide. Aluminum oxide can also be grey, white, or reddish-brown in color. Aluminum-oxide abra-

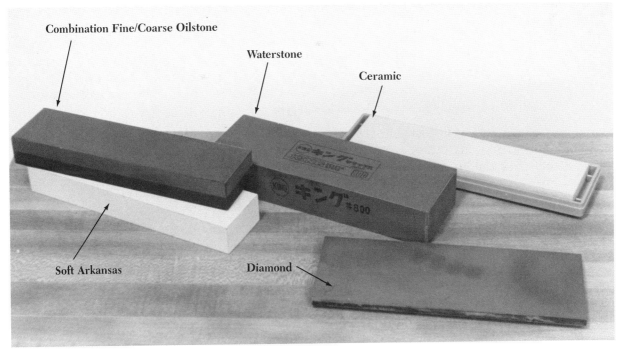

Illus. 1-3. *A variety of bench sharpening "stones."*

Natural or Arkansas stones vary in color from white to black. They are quarried in the state of Arkansas; hence their name. Natural oilstones are generally classified as hard or soft. Soft stones are more porous and cut faster than hard stones. Hard stones cut more slowly, but give more polished, keener edges. Some authorities claim that hard Arkansas stones produce the finest of all edges, and that these stones are the best choice among the abrasives for sharpening dental, medical, and other high-precision tools.

Aluminum-oxide and silicon-carbide oilstones are oil-filled by the manufacturer, and do not need to be soaked prior to first use. Natural stones are denser, do not absorb oil as fast, and thus are not oil-filled by the manufacturer.

Natural stones are essentially used to make the edge very keen after it has been worked with coarser aluminum-oxide or silicon-carbide stones. Natural stones are more expensive than man-made oilstones.

Oilstones in general are moderately expensive, wear slowly, and have a comparatively longer service life than waterstones. Because oilstones require oil as a lubricant, they are sometimes less preferred by some woodworkers who claim the oil contaminates their wood-project surfaces.

When using oilstones, wipe them frequently with a rag to prevent glazing and to remove worn abrasives and metal particles. Then give them a few drops of fresh oil.

Once an oil surface becomes worn or dished it is very difficult to reflatten. (See Illus. 1-4.) Re-flattening is a tedious job that can be done by rubbing the stone against a concrete surface, or against oil-lubricated glass or marble sprinkled with 60–80-grit silicon-carbide dust. Oilstones are best stored in covered, protective wood boxes. (See Illus. 1-5–1-7.)

Waterstones

Waterstones, also known as Japanese Waterstones, are also of either natural or man-made origin. (See Illus. 1-8.) Waterstones are quickly gaining popularity among progressive woodworkers. They cut much faster than typical oilstones.

Waterstones are quite porous and must be used with water as the lubricant and flushing agent. In fact, almost all waterstones must be soaked 5 to 10 minutes before use. Natural waterstones are very expensive and *should not* be soaked. Neither should the very-fine-grit stones (6000–8000 grit) that usually come pre-mounted onto wooden bases. Simply sprinkle these waterstones with water a few minutes before use and then intermittently during use.

Man-made waterstones are available in grit sizes that range from 100 to an ultra-fine, 8000 grit. Japanese waterstone grit designations do not correlate with the conventional United States grit designations. The chart on page 14 compares the Japanese and United States grit numbering systems and the range of designations for various types of abrasives.

Illus. 1-4. *You must true a dished or worn sharpening stone to be certain that it will sharpen well.*

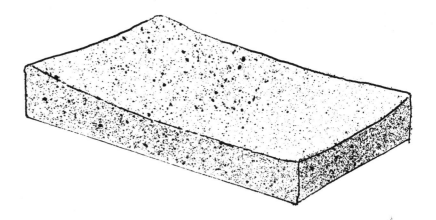

Illus. 1-5. *A shop-made sharpening-stone holder and storage box. To make such a box, chisel or rout out a recess ⅛ inch deep in a thick board. The board's base is made extra long, so that it can be clamped to the workbench.*

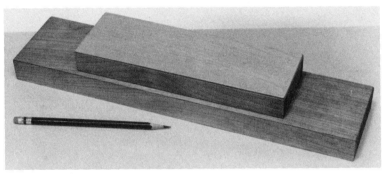

Illus. 1-6. *A covered box keeps shop dust and dirt off the sharpening stone.*

Illus. 1-7. *Another useful way to hold and support the oilstone is to rout or chisel a recess on the opposite side of the base, to hold and support the sharpening stone on its edge. This stone position is useful for certain jobs such as sharpening scrapers and shaper cutters.*

Illus. 1-8. *Waterstones can be soaked and stored in inexpensive plastic containers.*

ABRASIVE STONE TYPE	U.S. GRIT	JAPANESE GRIT
Coarse Silicone Carbide, Coarse Aluminum Oxide	100	150
Medium Silicon Carbide	180	240
Medium Aluminum Oxide, Coarse Diamond	240	280
Fine Silicon Carbide, Fine Aluminum Oxide	280	360
Medium Diamond	320	500
Washita	350	600
Soft Arkansas	500	1000–1200
Hard White Arkansas	700	2000
Fine Diamond, Medium Black Ceramic	600–700	2000
Hard Black Arkansas	900	4000
Ultra-Fine White Ceramic, Extra-Fine Diamond	1000–1200	6000

Waterstones should be kept well wetted during use. Water flushes away the metal filings and the worn or weakly bonded abrasive grains. This action exposes sharp, new edges and results in a fast cutting process. Decreasing pressure and allowing a build-up of slurry slows the abrasive rate, which, surprisingly, is a helpful practice in certain instances. (Slurry is a watery, mud-like mixture.) Utilizing the slurry with light pressure and less water enables you to work the somewhat more-worn abrasive grains to achieve a smoother polishing action than normal. Doing this just before switching to a finer-grit stone makes the transition more effective.

Because waterstones cut much faster than oilstones, they also wear down faster. This requires that you periodically flatten the waterstone to a true surface. You can flatten a fine-grit stone by rubbing it against a coarser one. Coarse stones can be flattened with 100–220 grit wet/dry silicon-carbide abrasive paper supported on any true surface such as plate glass or a flat-ground machine table or bed. (See Illus. 1-9.)

Various kinds of holders are available for waterstones. One simple shop-made holder suitable for basement shops with a nearby laundry tub or sink is shown in Illus. 1-10. A rubber floor mat placed on top of your work bench is another way to contain the mess that results from using a waterstone. A commerical combination storage and work area for waterstones is shown in Illus. 1-11.

One of the major advantages of waterstones is their fast cutting capabilities. This feature permits quick, cool removal of material to create

Illus. 1-9. *Flattening a glazed or worn waterstone by rubbing it over a 120-grit sheet of wet/dry silicon-carbide abrasive supported on a piece of plate glass. Water is the lubricant.*

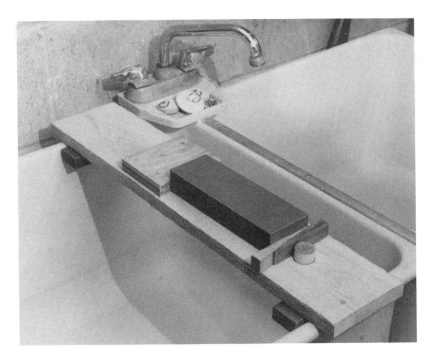

Illus. 1-10. This simple jig, made to bridge a laundry tub or sink, will contain the mess caused by using waterstones.

Illus. 1-11. With this commercial unit, you can store waterstones immersed in water simply by flipping the stone and clamps over when it is not being used. This unit comes with a tempered plateglass cover, and sheet abrasive for lapping or truing worn stones.

new bevels or to renew nicked edges. This class of work would normally be done with an electric dry grinder, which at best is difficult to use because of the tendency to overheat the edge of the tool.

Very-fine grit waterstones (6000 grit and finer) are available that are similar to 1200- to 1500-grit United States abrasives. These types of waterstones can be used to put a mirror-like finished edge on tools fairly quickly. (See Illus. 1-12.)

In addition to the mess associated with using waterstones, there are other disadvantages. Tools must be dried thoroughly after sharpening to prevent rusting. If the waterstones are used in unheated shops in northern climates, care must be taken to prevent them from freezing; otherwise, they will shatter. Remember, too, that you must diligently keep their surfaces flat and true, to prevent the stone from becoming worn and the obvious problems that condition would induce.

Waterstones are moderately priced, and a beginner can do a lot of tool sharpening with a pair of or a single combination stone with grits in the 800 to 4000 range.

Illus. 1-12. *This 8000-grit Japanese waterstone is used to add a final mirror-like finish to the tool's edge. It comes with a smaller Nagura stone for polishing the stone's surface. This smaller stone produces additional cutting paste on the surface.*

Ceramic Stones

Ceramic stones were until recently best known as the round, or triangular, rods used for sharpening kitchen knives. Lately, this hard, wear-resistant, and fast-cutting material has become available in 2×8-inch and smaller sizes, which are ideal for the woodworker.

Ceramic stones can be used to sharpen carbide cutters and router bits. They are made of aluminum-oxide abrasives (advertised as man-made sapphires) and baked at 3,000°F under pressure in a ceramic bonding agent. One of the best features of a ceramic stone is that is remains flat much longer than all other stones except diamond plates.

Ceramic stones do not require lubrication, which some authorities feel is vital for developing ultra-sharp edges. When used, the ceramic stone tends to load up quickly. This is because no lubricant or flushing agent is used with the stone, and it cuts quickly. You will have to clean the stone intermittently during lengthy sharpening sessions and after final use. Cleaning is quick and easy. Just use water, household detergent (cleanser), and a nylon dish pad (such as Scotch-Brite®).

Ceramic stones cost more per cubic inch of stone than most other types except diamonds. However, they are comparable in price on a stone-for-stone basis with all others except diamond plates.

Ceramic stones are no more brittle than other man-made or natural stones. They are highly preferred by wood-carvers requiring super-sharp edges.

Ceramic stones are available in either medium or fine grits. Manufacturers do not specify specific grit sizes but a fine-grit ceramic stone is comparable to a United States grit designation of approximately 1000 to 1200.

The same ceramic material in the form of small files approximately $1/4 \times 5$ inches and of round, triangular, square, and tear-drop cross sections is available for sharpening various drills, cutters and bits, including carbide router bits.

Diamond Sharpening Stones

Diamond sharpening stones, available in grit sizes of 600 and 1200 (United States), are called plates because the microscopic diamond crystals are bonded to flat, perforated, or solid-steel plates. (See Ilus. 1-13 and 1-14.) Some authorities claim that diamond stones never wear out or "dish" as other stones tend to do. Consequently, they always have a true, flat surface. In fact, diamond stones can be used to flatten all other sharpening stones because diamond is the hardest of any known material.

The hardness and enduring sharpness of diamond crystals make them ideal for fast, large-quantity metal removal when you are re-

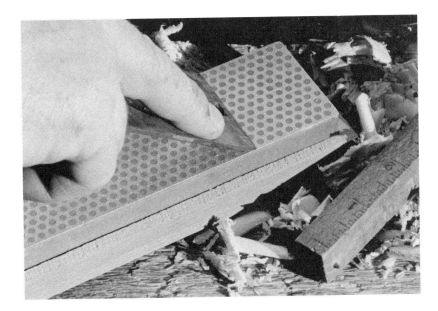

Illus. 1-13. *A perforated, diamond sharpening "stone." Micro-diamonds are partially embedded in nickel-plated perforated steel with round "islands" of tough plastic that act like the gullets of saw teeth to clear away the metal particles.*

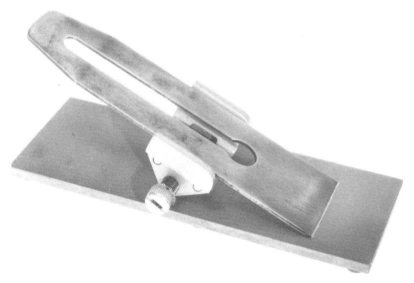

Illus. 1-14. *This type of diamond "stone" has its entire surface fully and evenly covered with diamond micro-crystals on a steel backing. Diamond stones never wear out or dish. Dishing commonly happens when sharpening guides, as shown, are used, because the entire surface area is not used equally.*

establishing bevels and reworking nicked edges. As a general rule, an increase in pressure will make diamond crystal stones cut more aggressively, and less pressure is advised when honing the final hedge.

Diamond stones require no liquid, but it is advisable to add a few drops of water to suspend and move away the metal filings. The surfaces can be easily cleaned with soap and water. The surfaces are non-corrosive (made of nickel and diamond), but metal filings left on moistened surfaces may leave brownish stains that look like but are not rust. Consequently, it is always a good idea to clean diamond stones immediately after using them.

The super-fine (1200-grit) diamond plate cuts a good final finish suitable for almost all wood-cutter sharpening jobs, including the hardest carbide tools. Because of the extreme sharpness of the ultra-fine diamond grits, the scratches produced are small but still visible. To achieve a smooth surface and remove even the finest scratches left with a super-fine diamond stone, use very light pressure and apply a liquid soap detergent, which will provide control over the cut, acting somewhat as a cushion. It feels like you're not cutting, but you are. A very smoothly polished surface is the result. However, I still prefer to follow the ultra-fine diamond with an 8000-grit waterstone when producing the ultimate polished edges on chisel and carving tools.

Diamond sharpening stones are more expensive than other types of stones. If you use these stones, you will get the flattest, truest and longest-lasting sharpening surface possible (that can also be easily cared for) and will be able to remove metal very quickly. Diamond slipstones, hones, and files of various shapes are also available. (See Illus. 1-15.)

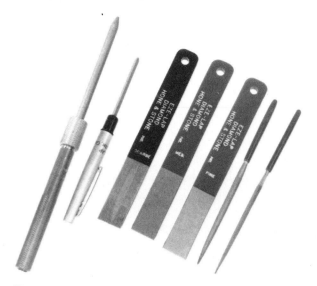

Illus. 1-15. *Various diamond-coated sharpening tools. On the left are rounds, in the center are pads or files, and on the right are needle files.*

Slipstones and Hones

Slipstones and hones are available in many different shapes to handle the contour of and any cutting-edge configuration imaginable. They are also available in all the same mediums as are the larger bench sharpening stones explored previously. Only a few of the most popular shapes and kinds are shown in Illus 1-16 and 1-17.

Files

Files are used to sharpen a number of wood-cutting tools. (See Illus. 1-18 and 1-19.) Conventional hardened steel files are used to sharpen the spurs and lips of boring tools, cabinet scrapers, saws, and similar tools made of softer steel. Diamond files and/or paddles and ceramics are used to sharpen harder materials, including carbides. (See Illus. 1-15.)

Strops

Traditional strops, such as the old barber's razor strop, are made of leather. (See Illus. 1-20.) You can make your own strop from any cowhide leather or similar scraps purchased from a leather craft store. You can also purchase commercial real-leather strops and new composition strops, as shown in Illus. 1-21 from mail-order houses.

Illus. 1-16. *A variety of slipstones and hones. From left to right: a set of four medium-grit aluminum-oxide slipstones; a 2×4-inch hard Arkansas tapered slip; a set of three water slipstones; a diamond-cone hone 4 inches long; and a flat, diamond honing stone.*

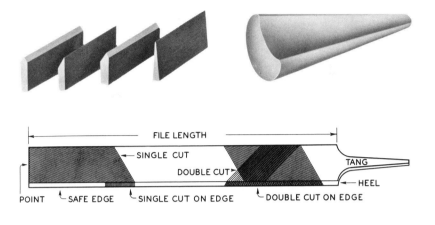

Illus. 1-17. *Far left: Small carving-tool slipstones. Left: A gouge slipstone.*

Illus. 1-18. *Top: Basic file nomenclature. Bottom: Basic file shapes.*

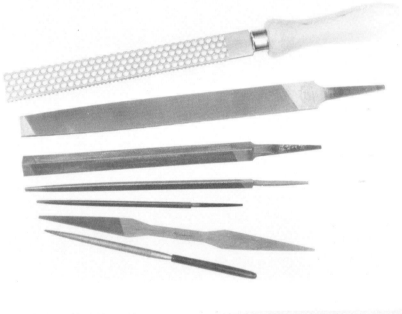

Illus. 1-19. *A selection of files used for sharpening various tools. From top to bottom: a perforated diamond all-purpose file, coarse (200 grit) on one side and fine (600 grit) on the other; a standard 8-inch single-cut mill file; a cant-saw file for sharpening in openings of less than 60 degrees; a 6-inch, slim three-square (triangular) file; a 4-inch extra-slim three-square file; a 7-inch auger bit file (one end with safe edges, and one end uncut to prevent damage to surfaces next to those being filed); and a half-round diamond needle file.*

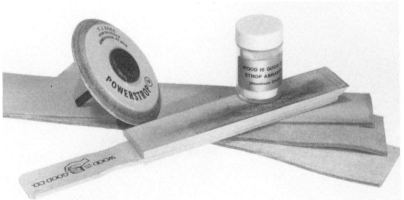

Illus. 1-20. *A variety of strops.*

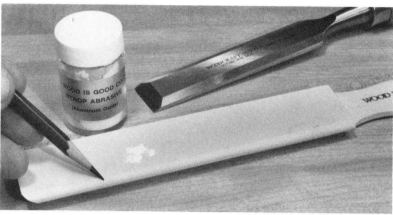

Illus. 1-21. *This composition strop has a round, bevelled edge for stropping the insides of gouges and V carving tools. If you strop tools lightly but regularly with a strop charged with a small amount of powdered aluminum oxide, they will stay very sharp.*

Honing Guides

Honing guides are almost essential for the beginner. (See Illus. 1-22–1-24.) A honing guide enables you to maintain the optimum required bevel on plane irons, chisels, and similar bevelled tools without effort. There are several types of honing guides available, but they all generally have the following features: (1) they can be adjusted for different kinds of tools; (2) they will support the tool as pre-adjusted to the stone to the bevel-angle desired; and (3) they have a roller that facilitates consistent, free movement or stroking of the tool over the surface of the stone.

Angle-Checking Devices

Angle-checking guides with triangular openings of various degrees or adjustable protractors may be useful to the tool-sharpening woodworker. (See Illus. 1-25.) They are particularly useful for checking sharpening bevels of chisels, plane irons, turning tools, twist drills, etc.

One simple way to check sharpening angles is to draw a series of lines on paper with a protractor, and then lay your tool on the lines to observe the angle.

Cleaning Brushes and Rakes

Cleaning brushes and rakes can be used to condition or remove filings, rust, etc., from hand and/or power sharpening tools. Some typical items are shown in Illus. 1-26.

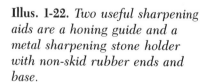

Illus. 1-22. *Two useful sharpening aids are a honing guide and a metal sharpening stone holder with non-skid rubber ends and base.*

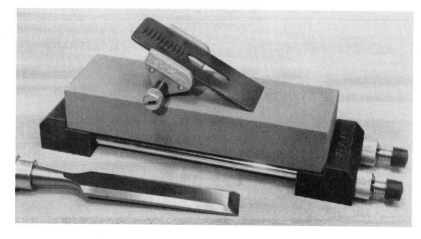

Illus. 1-23 (left). *One jaw in each set of jaws has a curved edge. This automatically keeps the tool or blade from twisting by pushing it flat against the straight jaw, which also automatically squares it to the stone.* **Illus. 1-24 (above).** *The honing guide with a chisel clasped in its special jaws. The guide will hold any tool from ¹⁄₁₆ to 3½ inches wide.*

Illus. 1-25. *A protractor with an adjustable locking arm is ideal for checking cutter angles.*

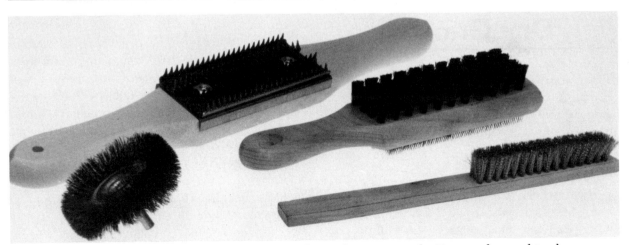

Illus. 1-26. *These tools can be used to clean and condition sharpening tools. Top: a rake, used to clean glazed, cloth buffing wheels. Left: an arbor-mounted wire wheel. Right-center: a file cleaner. Lower right: a brass wire brush.*

Chapter 2
SHARPENING MACHINES

This chapter explores a number of motor-driven grinding devices that can be categorized as either *dry* or *wet*. Power-driven strops, hones, and buffing devices are also included here.

Industry and most professional sharpening services have special equipment designed exclusively for sharpening one particular kind of tool or for one class of work. Flat jointer and planer knives, for example, are ground on a machine designed just for that job. The machines illustrated and described here that are suitable for the home shop are multi-purpose machines. They must be used to handle a variety of jobs and to sharpen many different woodworking tools. Some sharpening jobs are, therefore, more easily done than others, as you will learn in later chapters.

Dry Grinders

There are two basic types of dry grinders: wheel and abrasive belt grinders. Both kinds are available in different sizes. Most use silicon-carbide or aluminum-oxide abrasives.

Wheel Grinders

Vertical wheel grinders of the double-arbor type show in Illus. 2-1 and 2-2 are perhaps the most common and popular general-purpose grinder used in the workshop. The size of all wheel grinders is specified according to the maximum diameter of the wheels they are designed

to carry. Common home-shop wheel grinders range in size from 4 to 8 inches; 5- and 6-inch wheel grinders are the most common. Eight-inch grinders range in horsepower from 1/5 to 1.

Most inexpensive home-shop grinders rotate at 3450 rpm (revolutions per minute), which is generally too fast for casual sharpening of most home-shop woodworking tools. It is so easy to overheat and burn tool edges unless extreme care and a delicate, light touch is used.

The typical grinder is intended more for general grinding of yard and farm implements or general rough-metal work than for grinding delicate carving tool edges. There are grinders available for general tool sharpening that are of better quality and can be used at a slower speed than typical grinders, but these grinders are also more expensive. (See Illus. 2-3.)

Grinding Wheels. The most popular grinding wheels have silicon-carbide and aluminum-oxide abrasives. Most of the medium-to-lower-priced grinders come with low-quality, hard, slow-cutting medium-fine and medium-coarse wheels that are generally ineffective for tool sharpening. It would probably be better if grinders were sold without wheels or at least with wheels that would closer match the buyer's needs. Most grinding wheels that come with the machine should be replaced. Although many home-shop woodworkers do not like to change grinding wheels, different types of wheels, like circular-saw blades, should be used for different jobs. A multi-purpose grinding wheel simply will not do a good job at every single grinding job; it will do an average job at best.

Most woodworking tool experts recommend using a softer, more porous 60-to-100-grit white aluminum-oxide replacement wheel. This type of wheel will cut more rapidly with less frictional heat.

Specifying precise kinds and grades of grinding wheels involves a fairly complicated labelling system that is coded with various numbers and

Illus. 2-1. *A typical 6-inch (diameter of wheels), 3500 rpm utility bench grinder for the home shop. Note the small tool rests used to support the tool during grinding.*

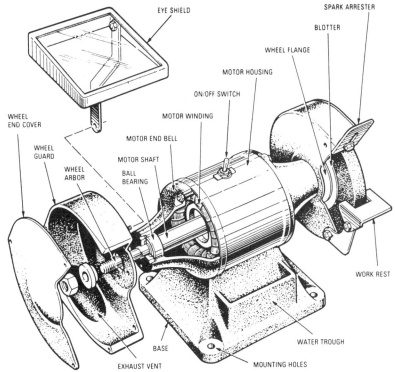

EYE SHIELD

SPARK ARRESTER

BLOTTER

WHEEL FLANGE

MOTOR HOUSING

ON/OFF SWITCH

MOTOR WINDING

WHEEL END COVER

MOTOR END BELL

WHEEL GUARD

MOTOR SHAFT

WHEEL ARBOR

BALL BEARING

WORK REST

BASE

EXHAUST VENT

MOUNTING HOLES

WATER TROUGH

Illus. 2-2. *A cutaway view of a bench grinder and its various functioning parts. The eye shield and other safety parts, which are attached to both sides of the grinder, are shown here on one side only.*

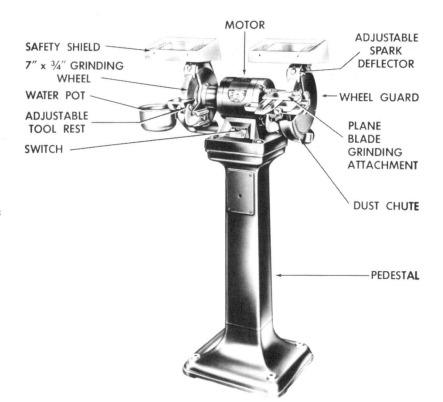

SAFETY SHIELD

7″ x ¾″ GRINDING WHEEL

WATER POT

ADJUSTABLE TOOL REST

SWITCH

MOTOR

ADJUSTABLE SPARK DEFLECTOR

WHEEL GUARD

PLANE BLADE GRINDING ATTACHMENT

DUST CHUTE

PEDESTAL

Illus. 2-3. *Delta's 7 inch, ½-horsepower pedestal tool-sharpening grinder is available in a choice of single-speed options: 1725, 2850, or 3450 rpm.*

letters. In addition to graded grit sizes, there are many different kinds of "bonds" that hold the abrasive particles together in their circular-wheel shape. These "bonds" include vitrified, silicate, and other type of bonds not of major interest or importance for the novice. Vitrified and silicate bonded wheels are appropriate for grinding edge tools.

Grinding wheels are also graded within the type of bond from hard to very soft. Hard wheels release their abrasive grains slowly, and tend to heat the tool and glaze more quickly than softer wheels. Soft wheels can be more easily sharpened.

Grinding wheels also have designations specifying porosity (space between abrasive grains). These designations range from dense to open. A porous wheel cuts more rapidly without excessive heating.

Grinding wheels operate safely at the speeds for which they were designed and manufactured. Each wheel carries its maximum speed designation printed on the blotter paper label. (See Illus. 2-6 and 2-7.)

Tool Rests.   The tool rests that come with most medium-to-low-cost home-shop grinders are frequently of poor construction, small, and are almost totally ineffective for the tool sharpener. Many tool rests are made of stamped metal and their supporting surfaces and edges are out of

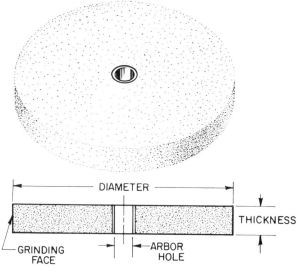

DIAMETER

THICKNESS

GRINDING FACE

ARBOR HOLE

Illus. 2-4. *Grinding wheel specifications and nomenclature.*

Illus. 2-5. *A selection of grinding wheels of different thicknesses and diameters. Most are variations of aluminum-oxide or silicon-carbide abrasive particles bonded together to circular disc shapes.*

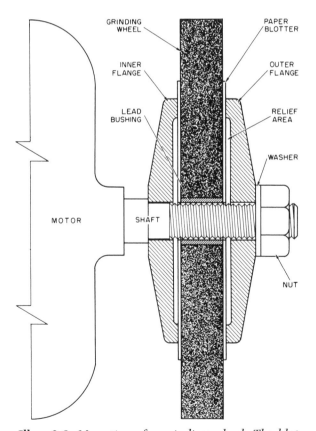

GRINDING WHEEL
PAPER BLOTTER
INNER FLANGE
OUTER FLANGE
LEAD BUSHING
RELIEF AREA
WASHER
MOTOR
SHAFT
NUT

Illus. 2-6. *Mounting of a grinding wheel. The blotter paper ensures even pressure on the wheel and dampens vibration between the wheel and shaft (arbor). The arbor nuts have appropriate left- and right-handed threads that tighten themselves against the rotation of the wheel.*

Illus. 2-7. *Changing a wheel. To tighten the right wheel, turn the right arbor nut clockwise. To tighten the left wheel, turn the arbor nut counter-clockwise. In both instances, you are turning opposite wheel rotation. Do not overtighten the nuts.*

alignment with the face axis of the wheel. This makes many freehand and guided grinding jobs frustrating and unnecessarily difficult.

One way to make grinding easier and more accurate is to devise your own tool rest. A typical example of a shop-made tool rest that can be

Illus. 2-8. *Better grinders have well-designed and sturdy tool rests. The tool rest on this grinder is fully adjustable and supports each side of the wheel.*

adapted to most 6 to 8-inch bench grinders is shown in Illus. 2-9–2-12. Suggested construction details are given in Illus. 2-13. The tool rest shown in Illus. 2-13 utilizes carriage bolts in slotted wood and wing-nut adjustments. This system should also incorporate regular washers that have lock washers or regular nuts that can be tightened securely with a standard wrench. Once this tool rest is properly adjusted and secured, a wide range of sharpening jobs can be more easily done. In fact, some auxiliary jigs such as the one shown in Illus. 2-10 will ensure maximum control and accuracy when they have a good, true edge to work off.

Truing and Dressing Grinding Wheels. Grinding wheels, like other cutting tools, need frequent maintenance to function efficiently. "Truing" is balancing the wheel so that it runs concentric to the arbor without wobbling or vi-

Illus. 2-9. *A modified grinder setup. Note that the grinder is bolted to a base, which, in turn, is clamped to the workbench. The shop-made, long, adjustable tool rest makes it easier and safer to grind most tools.*

Illus. **2-10.** *This commercially available grinding jig ensures complete control and accuracy when used with the shop-made tool rest.*

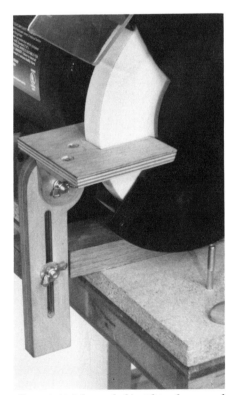

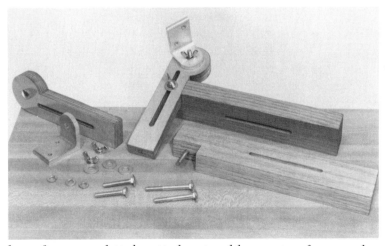

Illus. 2-11 (**above left**). *This shop-made tool rest features a slotted vertical post-and-base system for up-and-down and in-and-out adjustments, and a pivoting plate that gives support at the desired angle.* **Illus. 2-12** (**above right**). *The basic components for making the tool rest shown in Illus. 2-9–2-11. Carriage bolts 1½ and 2 inches in length, and lock washers under wing nuts, ensure that tight adjustments can be made.*

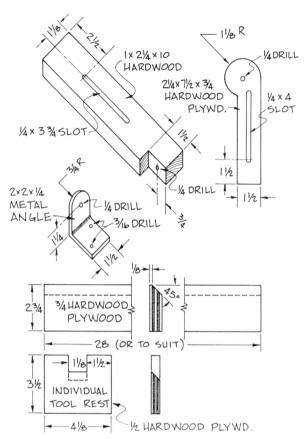

Illus. 2-14. *A glazed wheel may have visible metal particles embedded in its surface.*

Illus. 2-13. *Typical construction details for making your own tool rest.*

brating. "Dressing" is cleaning up the working surface of the wheel. Dressing removes a "glazed" surface and breaks away dull abrasive grains. (See Illus. 2-14.) A glazed wheel is often embedded with metal particles. This condition creates excessive grinding heat when metal rubs over metal. Dressing also is done to make the face of the wheel flat to cut away worn grooves and irregularities, or to give the face an entirely new, specific shape for specialized grinding jobs. (See Illus. 2-15.)

Wheel Dressers. Different kinds of wheel dressing tools are shown in Illus. 2-16. They are all designed to wear away the face of the wheel. A star-wheel dresser cuts fast and leaves a coarse, aggressive-cutting wheel. (See Illus. 2-16 and 2-17.) Abrasive wheel and stick dressers cut more slowly, and are more efficient when used to re-

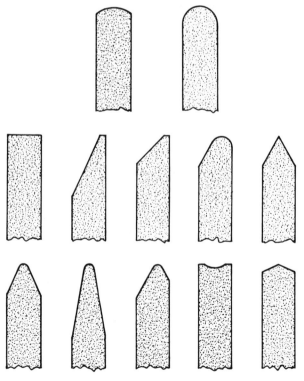

Illus. 2-15. *You can purchase grinding wheels or dress them yourself to special shapes for any grinding requirement.*

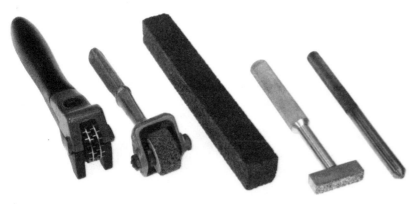

Illus. 2-16. *Various kinds of wheel dressers. From left to right: a star-wheel, an abrasive wheel, a silicon-carbide stick, a diamond T-bar, and a single-point diamond.*

Illus. 2-17. *Using a star-wheel dresser to true the face of the wheel.*

condition the surfaces to improve abrasive cutting action, rather than for truing or heavy stone removal. They also give the wheel a finer grind.

Diamond-T bar dressers, which have multiple embedded diamonds, are easy to use, but are expensive. A single diamond-point dresser is preferred by many, but this type of dresser has to be moved very carefully and uniformly across the surface of the wheel.

Illus. 2-18 and 2-19 show a single clamp-and-guide jig that can be used with a single-point diamond dresser. The depth of cut and the speed at which you move a single-point diamond across the wheel affects the coarseness or fineness of the grinding surface. (See Illus. 2-20.) Light and slow dressing cuts will produce a finer cutting surface, but also one more likely to burn the tool's cutting edge.

Almost all wheel manufacturers do not recommend grinding on the side of the wheel. However, many very light grinding jobs can be done if you use common sense. For example, obviously, don't grind on the sides of thin wheels. Sometimes a very light side-wheel dressing will

make the wheels run truer, giving grinders less overall vibration. (See Illus. 2-21.) *Note:* Always observe and read safety instructions and study owner's manuals before doing any work on power-tool grinders.

Illus. 2-18. *A holder-guide for a single-point diamond wheel dresser.*

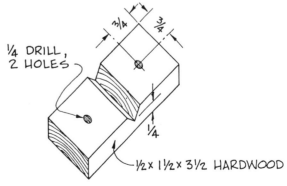

Illus. 2-19. *Detail for making a holder-guide for a single-point diamond wheel dresser.*

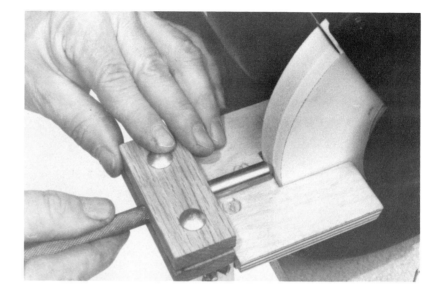

Illus. 2-20. *Dressing the face of the wheel.*

Illus. 2-21. *Dressing the side of the wheel. Take very light cuts.*

Chillers and other power tools. As mentioned earlier, high-speed dry grinders can overheat and ruin the tool's cutting edge. Most dry-grinding requires a very light touch and frequent dipping of the tool into a cooling bath of water. Some woodworkers use a hand-operated misting system such as the type used to clean windows or to pump moisture particles to house plants. However, this method is dangerous because you will not be able to control the tool with both hands, and flying water particles can become messy if sufficient cooling is to take place directly at the point of the grinding action.

One handy device to have around the shop is a "spot chiller." This is a vortex-tube generator that operates with compressed air. (See Illus. 2-22 and 2-23.) This unusual device has no moving parts, requires no maintenance, and provides a continuous and instantaneous stream of very cold, clean air (50–70°F colder than the inlet supply air).

A spot chiller will minimize micro-chip cracking and burning of a tool edge when you are dry-grinding. It is most effective when used with 80 to 100 PSI (pounds per square inch) of pressure. Vortex-tube chillers are fairly expensive; they are about equal to the cost of a medium-priced home-shop grinder.

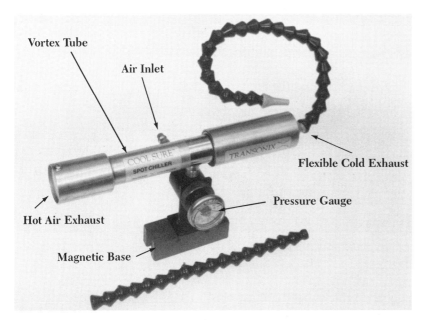

Vortex Tube

Air Inlet

Flexible Cold Exhaust

Hot Air Exhaust

Pressure Gauge

Magnetic Base

Illus. 2-22. *This vortex-tube spot chiller makes an effective but fairly expensive grinder accessory. It provides cool air when dry-grinding that practically eliminates all possibilities of burning or overheating.*

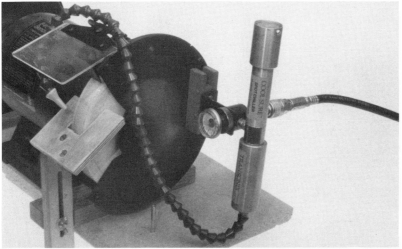

Illus. 2-23. *A spot chiller set up for cool dry-grinding. The magnetic base attaches to the wheel cover. Cold air is directed through the flexible plastic tubing to the grinding area.*

Chillers are also ideal for drilling plastics and metals. Various chillers are available from Transonix Corp. of Lowell, MA.

Other hand-held or stationary power tools can easily be adapted to handle a variety of tool-sharpening jobs. Some examples include hand drills, rotary tools, drill presses, table saws, lathes, and some sanding machines. Small abrasives mounted on spindles or shanks are useful for sharpening many workshop cutting tools ranging from small carving burrs to jointer knives. (See Illus. 2-24–2-28.)

Illus. 2-24. *Mounted grinding wheels have shanks or arbors that fit into chucks or collets.*

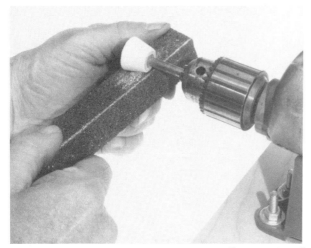

Illus. 2-25 and 2-26. *Dressing a mounted wheel with an abrasive stick.*

Illus. 2-27. *Small mounted wheels made of aluminum-oxide, silicon-carbide, and even diamond-coated abrasives are available for use with rotary power tools.*

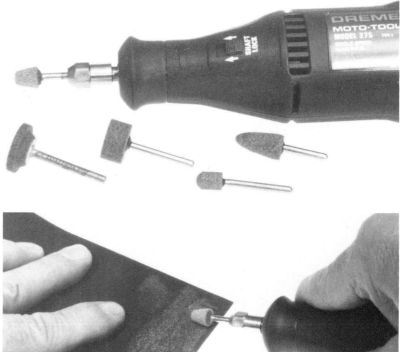

Illus. 2-28. *Dressing the shape of a small mounted wheel with a piece of silicon-carbide abrasive paper.*

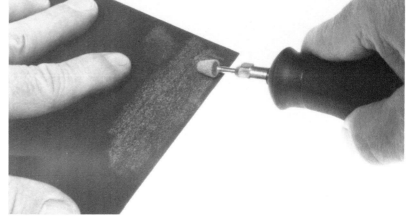

Illus. 2-29 and 2-30 show various grinding, buffing, and polishing wheels that can be mounted to arbors. Use them to convert other power tools and unused motors into very effective power sharpening machines. (See Illus. 2-31–2-36.)

Illus. 2-29. *An assortment of polishing, buffing, and stropping wheels. In the back row, from left to right: a 5-inch-diameter nylon mesh wheel impregnated with abrasive grit; a 6-inch-diameter sewn cotton buffing wheel; a 6-inch-diameter × ¾-inch-thick hard-felt wheel; and a 6-inch-diameter × ¾-inch-thick rubberized wheel. In the front are two 3½-inch-diameter rotary leather strops.*

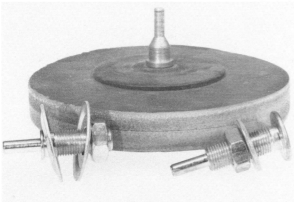

Illus. 2-30. *Arbors with flanges are available to carry wheels, buffers, or abrasives of any kind for sharpening and polishing in power-driven chucks such as those on a drill press.*

Illus. 2-32. *A fast-cutting rubberized polishing wheel being used in a drill press. This wheel comes in four grits: coarse, medium, fine, and extra fine. It is made of silicon carbide bonded with chemical rubber, which provides a unique cushioning abrasive action.*

Illus. 2-31 (left). *This inexpensive plastic drill stand, with clamp, quickly converts a hand drill into a power sharpening machine. Here a leather strop that is mounted to a round arbor is being chucked in the drill.*

Illus. 2-33. *Threaded motor-arbor adapters permit you to mount any kind of wheel to any spare motor. Be sure to purchase adapters with right- or left-hand threads that tighten against the motor's rotational direction.*

Illus. 2-34. *An old pump motor with a 6-inch-diameter × ¾-inch-thick hard-felt wheel is ideal for polishing carving tools and knife bevels.*

Illus. 2-35. *Just a few of many different polishing compounds available that come in bar and stick forms.*

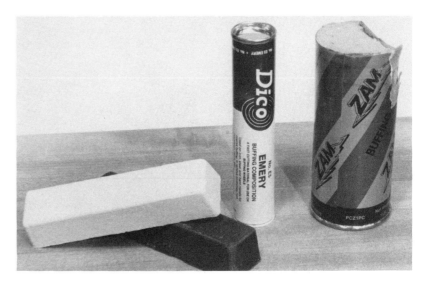

Illus. 2-36. *Loading (charging) a hard-felt wheel with polishing compound.*

Abrasive Belt Grinders

Abrasive belt grinders have belts that range from 1–6 inches wide, and of the type used to sand wood. (See Illus. 2-37 and 2-38.) They can also be used for workshop sharpening jobs.

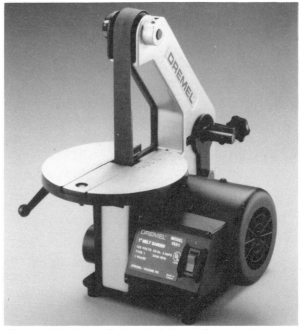

Illus. 2-38. *Dremel's 1-inch belt sander can be used for tool-sharpening jobs involving grinding and even polishing operations.*

Illus. 2-37. *Delta's basic 1-inch belt sander/grinder shown without motor or base.*

The belts on these grinders cut cooler than bonded abrasive wheels, though you must still be careful not to overheat them. Because long belts have more square inches of sharpening area, they do not glaze as quickly as wheel grinders. Another advantage is that abrasive belt grinders do not need to be trued or dressed.

Light-duty belt grinders tend to vibrate, and are difficult to "tune" for precision-grinding of wide knives or blades such as plane irons. Usually the tables are not designed to adjust or tilt sufficiently to make basic bevel grinds. Wide belts must be well-tensioned, and must move over the back-up platten flatly. Otherwise, grinding will be counterproductive, particularly when grinding plane irons, chisels, and tools with similar edges.

Because of the inherent design of abrasive belt grinders in general, they are ideal for sharpening certain workshop tools. Handled drawknives, wood-turning scraping tools, and some narrow chisels, carving knives, and drilling/boring tool points can often be handled more easily on belt sanders than on high-speed dry wheel grinders. Dremel even offers a buffing belt for polishing tool bevels and other jobs. (See Illus. 2-39.)

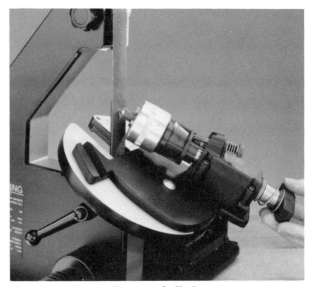

Illus. 2-40. *Dremel's twist-drill sharpening accessory attaches to its 1-inch belt sander table. This accessory will sharpen drill bits from ⅛ to ½ inch in diameter.*

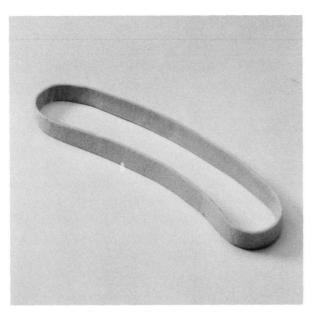

Illus. 2-39. *A buffing belt accessory for Dremel's 1-inch belt sander. This belt can be charged with buffing compound and used to polish all tool bevels and edges in the same manner as a buffing wheel.*

Drill Sharpeners. Dremel makes a drill-bit grinding accessory for its 1-inch belt sander. (See Illus 2-40.) Two special grinders for sharpening drill bits are shown in Illus. 2-41 and 2-42. One is driven by its own internal motor. The other is an accessory powered by an electric drill. These special sharpening tools are very helpful if you have many dull or broken bits.

Illus. 2-41. *The Martek drill-bit sharpener is powered by a portable electric drill. It will sharpen all bits from 1/16 to ⅜ inch in diameter.*

Illus. 2-42. *Black & Decker's electric drill-bit sharpener will resharpen carbon and high-speed bits from ⅛ to ⅜ inch in diameter.*

Wet Sharpening Machines

Wet sharpening machines incorporate a water or oil bath or coolant feeding system at the grinding area that prevents the tool from overheating and minimizes wheel load up. Home-shop wet-grinders utilize water as the coolant. There are several types in a broad range of prices available for the home shop. Some are examined below.

Sears Wet Sharp Machine

The Sears Wet Sharp Machine is a small, inexpensive, light-duty sharpening machine. (See Illus. 2-43.) It features a capillary wheel wetting action. A felt wiper "pulls" water from a small reservoir under the tool rest. This wets the wheel while simultaneously wiping it clean of grinding residue. (See Illus. 2-44.) This machine should only be used to do very light grinding on small tools.

One of the most unusual features of the Sears Wet Sharp Machine is the built-in guide for scissor sharpening. (See Illus. 2-45.) The surface of the moulded plastic housing just above the wheel slants at the perfect angle for grinding scissors.

Illus. 2-43. *The Sears Wet Sharp Machine.*

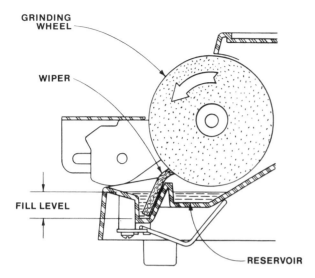

Illus. 2-44. *A sectional view showing the functioning components of the Sears Wet Sharp Machine.*

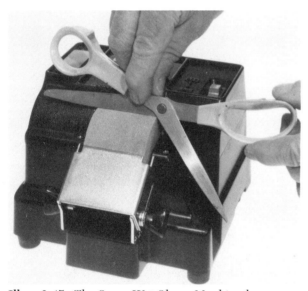

Illus. 2-45. *The Sears Wet Sharp Machine has a scissors-sharpening guide built into the housing above the wheel. Simply holding the scissors against the housing assures the operator of the correct grinding angle. The scissors are slowly drawn across the wheel to complete the job.*

Delta Wet/Dry Grinder

Delta's Wet/Dry Grinder has two aluminum-oxide wheels powered by the same 1/5-horse-power motor. (See Illus. 2-46.) This machine

incorporates a worm-gear and shaft-drive mechanism that rotates its two wheels at different speeds. The machine features a conventional 5-inch-diameter dry-running, 3450 rpm grinder, and a 10-inch-diameter × 2-inch-wide wheel that rotates at just 70 rpm through a water reservoir. The small, high-speed wheel is used for many common home-shop grinding jobs. The large, wet, and slow-moving wheel is ideal for sharpening and honing hard tools without overheating and damaging their temper. Plane irons, chisels, knives, and carving and lathe tools, among many other tools, can be given a final keen edge. The wet end of the machine features a well-designed, very functional tool rest that incorporates a cross-slide angle guide. (See Illus. 2-47.)

Waterstone Sharpeners

Makita's Model 9820 sharpener has features similar to several other Japanese-made motorized waterstone machines available today. (See Illus. 2-48.) These include the Rakuda and Matsunaga machines. All these waterstone machines have one-speed horizontal waterstones that rotate at approximately 500–550 rpm, and gravity-fed, water-reservoir cooling systems. Most have an adjustable angle guide that allows you to grind jointer and hone planer knives. The machines also come with a 1000-grit stone, but 6000 grit stones are also available. The circular stones of all the machines are approximately 1 inch thick by 8 inches in diameter.

The wheels can be changed quickly and simply. Highland Hardware of Atlanta, Georgia has an optional, 120-grit green wheel available exclusively for the Makita sharpener. This wheel is recommended for very fast, aggressive grinding of all metals, including carbide.

The Makita sharpener, when fitted with the coarse green stone, can handle every level of woodworking knife- and blade-sharpening needs. Severely nicked jointer knives, for example, can be quickly reground without fear of overheating.

The Makita sharpener can also be used to give any tool an ultra-sharp polished edge for tough cutting jobs (like planing curly or bird's-eye ma-

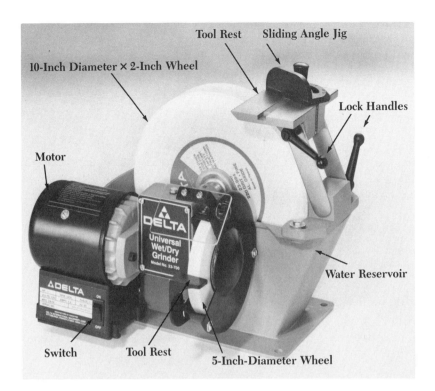

Tool Rest

Sliding Angle Jig

10-Inch Diameter × 2-Inch Wheel

Lock Handles

Motor

Water Reservoir

Switch

Tool Rest

5-Inch-Diameter Wheel

Illus. 2-46. *Delta's Universal Wet/Dry Grinder.*

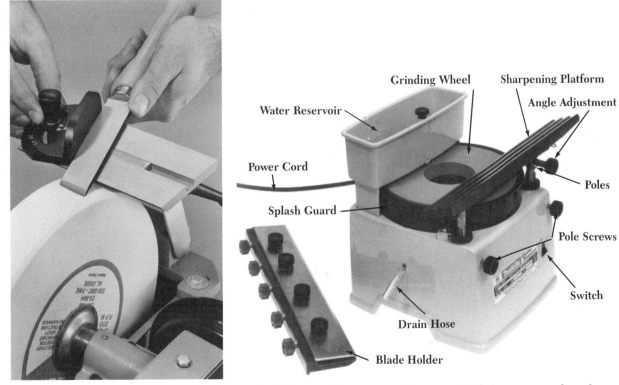

Grinding Wheel

Sharpening Platform

Water Reservoir

Angle Adjustment

Power Cord

Poles

Splash Guard

Pole Screws

Switch

Drain Hose

Blade Holder

Illus. 2-47 (above left). *A close-up look at the sliding angle jig as used here to grind the compound angles required on a skew wood-turning chisel.* Illus. 2-48 (above right). *The basic components of Makita's model 9820 motorized waterstone sharpener.*

ple) with just a quick wheel change. Individual long tools like planer blades up to 16-inches long or tools with extra-wide edges can be more accurately ground and sharpened in the home shop with this type of equipment than by any other process.

Because motorized waterstones do cut quickly, make sure that the angle is set correctly at the start. (See Illus. 2-49.) Though these machines are power-driven, and usually jig-guided, operator skill and coordination does play a significant role in their successful use. It does take time and effort to learn how to adjust and use these machines. They are also messy, especially when used to grind long knives that extend beyond the edge of the wet, rotating wheel.

Major differences among motorized waterstone machines lie primarily in the quality of their combination tool rest knife grinding guides. The better ones are made of solid, heavy cast iron. The poorer quality ones are simply made from formed sheet metal.

In addition to guided sharpening jobs, these machines are also very suitable for freehand grinding and honing. (See Illus. 2-50.)

Illus. 2-49. *Adjusting the sharpening platform guide to the desired angle. Turning this adjustment screw clockwise lowers the platform, making the sharpening angle more acute.*

Illus. 2-50. *Sharpening a gouge freehand with the sharpening platform guide removed from the machine. (Photo courtesy of Highland Hardware)*

Chapter 3

SAFETY TECHNIQUES

Woodworkers should always take the necessary steps to prevent accidents when using sharpening machines and when sharpening by hand. Hand-sharpening edge tools is sometimes more dangerous than actually using the tool. Remember when cutting wood to keep both hands behind the cutting edge of the tool and to direct all cutting strokes away from one's own body.

When using bench or honing stones, it's also safer to keep both hands on the tool and move the tool over the stone. This is safer than holding the tool stationary with one hand while moving the stone over it with the other. When it is necessary to do the latter, always try to stroke off or away from the cutting edge, rather than into it. (See Illus. 3-1.)

Feeling an Edge

It is often advantageous to feel for a burr or wire edge at various stages of sharpening. Woodworkers seem to have many foolish ways of touching an edge to test it for sharpness. Some try to determine if the edge is sharp by shaving hair off their arms, or by even cutting whiskers from their face and throat! Other, more conservative souls make various fingernail tests. Running the pad of your finger along the edge is also foolish. There is only one safe way to touch a cutting

edge with the pad of one's fingers. This is shown in Illus. 3-2 and 3-3.

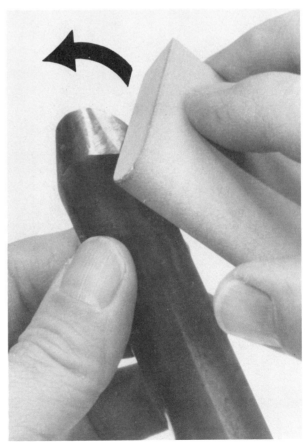

Illus. 3-1. *Honing the outside bevel of a turning gouge. Stroke the stone off and away from the edge, not towards it.*

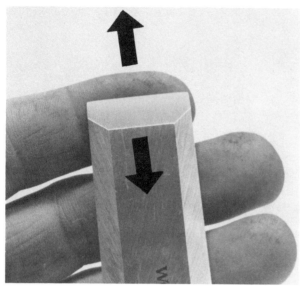

Illus. 3-2. *The only proper way to touch or feel an edge. Very lightly move your finger in a direction that is across at a right angle to the cutting edge, as shown. Never move your finger parallel with or along the edge.*

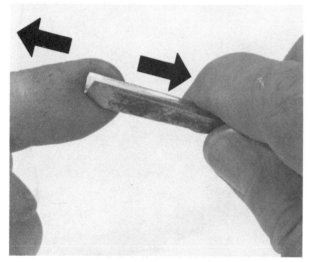

Illus. 3-3. *The only way to touch or feel an edge. The finger is very lightly moved past the cutting edge as the tool is simultaneously moved away.*

Using a Grinder Safely

Whenever changing the cutting instrument on any power cutting tool, unplug the tool from the power source. In the case of a grinder, unplug the grinder cord when changing grinding wheels. Other safety precautions are as follow:

1. Study the owner's manual.

2. Do not use cracked or chipped wheels.

3. Ensure that loose clothing does not come into contact with the revolving work. Never wear gloves or jewelry or hold work with a rag. These items can get caught in the wheel and cause serious injury.

4. Use only grinders that have wheels enclosed in hood-type guards.

5. Do not exceed the rotational speed limits of wheels, buffers, etc., as specified on the wheel by the manufacturer or on the package the wheel comes in. (See Illus. 3-4.)

Illus. 3-4. *Do not exceed the maximum rotational speed limits for grinding wheels and buffers as specified on the wheel itself (as shown on the right) or on the manufacturer's packaging (as shown at the left).*

6. Keep the tool rest adjusted ⅛ to ¹⁄₁₆ inch from the face of the grinding wheel. (See Illus. 3-5). Too much clearance may permit work to jam between the wheel and the tool rest.

Illus. 3-5. *Adjust the tool rest on the grinder so that it is very close to the face of the wheel, as shown, but never touches it.*

Illus. 3-6. *These impact goggles fit snugly against the face and have an elastic strap and air vents for comfort.*

7. Make adjustments only when the power is off and the tool is unplugged.

8. Make sure that the adjustment bolts and nuts are tight. Check them frequently.

9. Always wear goggles with side shields or a suitable wrap-around face shield. (See Illus. 3-6 and 3-7.)

10. Keep the eyeshields of the grinder in place while using it.

11. Stand to one side, away from the line of the wheel(s), when turning on the power. If a wheel is faulty, centrifugal force may cause it to break.

12. Do heavy grinding on the face of the wheel only, not on the side of the wheel. Side-wheel work should be limited to very light grinding, and should never be done with thin wheels.

13. Make sure that bench grinders are bolted or clamped securely.

14. Dress and true wheels at first sign of wobble or vibration.

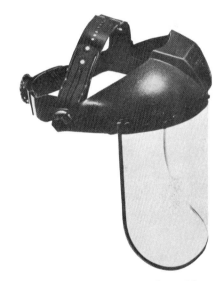

Illus. 3-7. *This face shield has an adjustable headband. The shield can be lifted up out of the way when you are not grinding.*

15. Wear a dust mask during extended periods of grinding for protection from very fine microscopic grinding particles.

16. Move the work from side to side over the face of the wheel to distribute wear and minimize heat build-up.

17. Do not touch the ground surface immediately after sharpening; it may be extremely hot.

18. Cool the tool by dipping it into water frequently.

19. From time to time remove the wheel cover guards and clean away any impacted grinding dust.

20. Do not force grinding. Always bring the work into wheel contact with a slow, smooth motion.

21. Never leave the grinder unattended. Turn off the power if not using the grinder.

22. When installing new belts on a belt grinder, make sure that they will run in the direction recommended by the manufacturer.

23. Always rotate powered leather strops, felt and fabric buffing wheels, and rubberized abrasive wheels *away* from the tool's cutting edge. (See Illus. 3-8.) If not, the tool will bite into the rotating wheel, creating a very hazardous situation.

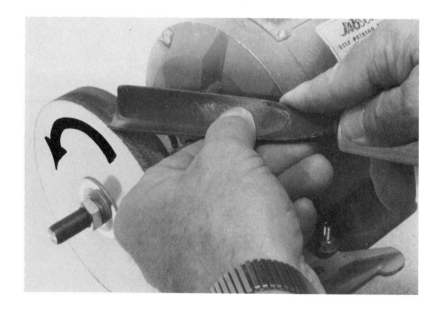

Illus. 3-8. *"Soft" polishing wheels, such as power-driven leather strops, fabric buffing wheels, rubberized abrasive wheels, and this hard-felt wheel* must rotate away *from the tool's cutting edge, as shown here.*

Chapter 4

CLEANING TOOLS

Keeping cutting tools clean is as important as keeping them sharp. It takes so little time and effort to wipe a tool clean and apply lubricant or a coating to protect and preserve it. (See Illus. 4-1.) Many woodworkers are not aware of the problems stemming from using dirty tools until it is too late. Sharp, but dirty, tools often cut as if they are just half-sharp. A tool that has pitch and resin deposits, is slightly corroded, or has rusty or tarnished surfaces will not be able to remove chips as easily and will undergo unnecessary heat

build-up. (See Illus. 4-2.) Tool clearances become reduced, chip removal is slowed, and tool temperatures increase. Heat accelerates tool dulling.

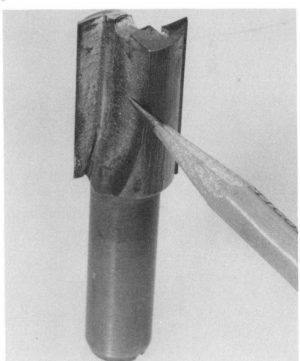

Illus. 4-2. *Deposits of gum or pitch will accumulate quickly on bits and cutters when they are used to cut certain resinous woods such as pine, redwood, and cedar.*

Illus. 4-1. *Just a few of many products to help clean and maintain tools. Lubricate tool surfaces after cleaning (and sharpening) to prevent rusting and to reduce resin accumulation. New, dry lubricants minimize friction by lowering cutting temperatures, thus preventing the tool from becoming dull prematurely.*

Resin and pitch are sticky substances secreted by the wood; some species of wood secrete more resin and pitch than others. Pine, redwood, cedar, basswood, and soft or moist woods in general are more of a problem than most hardwoods. Resinous deposits can build up surprisingly quick on the face or cutting side of bits, blades, and teeth where the tool contacts the cut chips and shavings. This condition makes it more difficult for the cutting tools to quickly and cleanly remove chips and shavings.

Frictional heat is generated when the chips or shavings are not removed as quickly from the cutting area as intended by the design of the tool. The chips and shavings are recut again and again. As the tool gets hotter, the tars and pitch harden and build up, and are glazed or baked onto the surfaces of the tool. The heat quickly dissipates to the thinnest metal part of the tool—the cutting edge.

Cleaning Techniques

Remove anything foreign to the surfaces of the tool before sharpening it. If you do not, pitch and resin on the tool will clog your sharpening stone or sharpening tool's surface. Soon the abrasives will become glazed, and the tool will become unnecessarily hot. (See Illus. 4-3–4-6.)

There are many commercially available tool-cleaning products that are touted as high-performance cleaners. Oven cleaner in spray or gel form is one type that does an excellent job of

Illus. 4-3. *Cleaning a bit. Oven cleaner is being applied liberally to all its surfaces.*

Illus. 4-4. *Allow the cleaner to penetrate and cut through the resinous film for 5 to 20 minutes, depending upon the condition of the tool. Brush and wipe the cleaner off.*

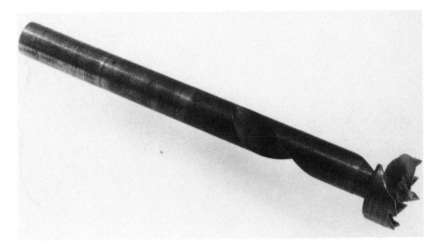

Illus. 4-5. *A dirty multi-spur bit with a film of pitch and residue accumulated over a period of time from boring resinous woods.*

Illus. 4-6. *The bit after being cleaned with just oven cleaner.*

removing pitch and resin. However, solvents other than oven cleaner can be used. Hot water used with detergent or ammonia will sometimes work. Turpentine, paint, and lacquer thinners are fairly aggressive solvents that are more dangerous to use.

Do not use tools with hard edges such as chisels, scrapers, and screwdrivers to chip away at crusted deposits. You will put scratches in surfaces you really want to keep smooth and polished to minimize such adhesions.

Tools that are not used and are not protected will also develop microscopic coatings of tarnish or rust, because their surfaces are subject to the moisture in the air. These types of problems are more prevalent in unheated workshops, basements, or garage shops where environmental humidity is high. Tools that have even slightly corroded metal surfaces will have a greater build-

up of resin when used than clean, polished, and lubricated tools.

Rubbing surfaces with steel wool, abrasive-impregnated fabrics, or sheet abrasives will quickly clean slightly tarnished surfaces. (See Illus. 4-7.) Power-driven wire brushes and soft abrasive-impregnated fabric wheels are ideal for many such jobs. (See Illus. 4-8.)

Advanced stages of rust on tool surfaces cause pitting of the metal. It is impossible to fully or properly sharpen any tool that has a pitted surface. Deep surface pitting at or near the cutting edge shows up as chip-like nicks as the tool is ground back during sharpening. (See Illus. 4-9.) Pitted and irregular surfaces must not only be removed, they must be completely flattened before effective sharpening can ever begin. (See Illus. 4-10.)

Pitting on tools with large surfaces, such as

Illus. 4-7. *Use 320- to 600-grit abrasive paper (silicon carbide) wrapped around a dowel to clean away film or residue on the inside surfaces of gouges and similar tools before sharpening them.*

Illus. 4-8. *Using an abrasive-impregnated nylon fibre-mesh wheel to polish a plane iron cap; this prevents rusting and minimizes surface friction with the shaving.*

Illus. 4-9. *A severely pitted chisel back. It will be impossible to give this tool a well-sharpened edge until the surface is ground flat and smooth. If not, the deep pits will show up as chip-like nicks at the cutting edge as the bevel side is ground.*

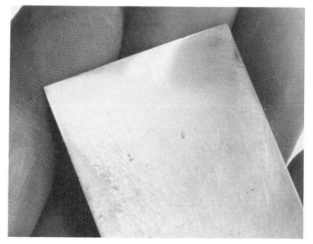

Illus. 4-10. *After much work, most of the pitting is removed except for those deep areas indicated by the dark spots. Note the scratches on the surface remaining from the coarse abrasives.*

hand saws, saw blades, plane irons, jointer knives, *cannot* be removed easily in the home shop. In many cases, the surfaces need to be ground professionally with special machines called surface grinders. This will probably cost more than a new replacement tool. You can attempt to wear down pitted surfaces yourself, by hand, by beginning with a coarse stone, and then following with successively finer grits until the surface finish is sufficiently restored and polished.

Do not try to use a conventional dry grinder to clean or resurface the pitted surfaces of chisels or plane irons. It's impossible to get perfectly flat, true surfaces. You should be able to do minimal surface-grinding on a motorized waterstone, but this is slightly more difficult than might be imagined. The resulting surfaces must be perfectly flat. A surface that is not completely flat will create subsequent sharpening problems.

The following two chapters cover the techniques for flattening the backs of plane irons and chisels.

Chapter 5
CHISELS

The wood chisel is an easy tool to sharpen. Once you learn to effectively sharpen a chisel, the same general principles can be applied to sharpen other single-bevel edge tools. Two important points vital to chisel-sharpening are:

1. Do not allow the tool to overheat during grinding. If the edge quickly discolors to a deep blue, it has been overheated. All of the discolored metal must be ground away more carefully than previously so it isn't overheated a second time.

2. A chisel must have a perfectly flat and true back to cut effectively. The back is the surface opposite the bevel side. (See Illus. 5-1 and 5-2.)

Bevels

Chisels can be ground to any one of a variety of different bevel angles, depending upon the kind of chisel or the type of work you intend to do with it. (See Illus. 5-3.) The precise bevel angle is not essential for the beginning woodworker. Try for a primary bevel angle of approximately 25 degrees, which is good for general-purpose work. (See Illus. 5-4.) Another option is to simply grind the chisel to the existing bevel.

Chisels have one primary bevel that can be either *flat* or *hollow-ground*. (See Illus. 5-1.) Flat bevels result from the following: 1) hand-grinding with one of the various bench stones; 2) grinding

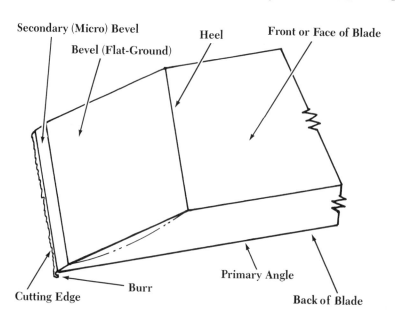

Illus. 5-1. *Terms associated with sharpening chisels and similar single-bevel hand tools, including plane blades (irons).*

Secondary (Micro) Bevel

Bevel (Flat-Ground)

Heel

Front or Face of Blade

Primary Angle

Back of Blade

Burr

Cutting Edge

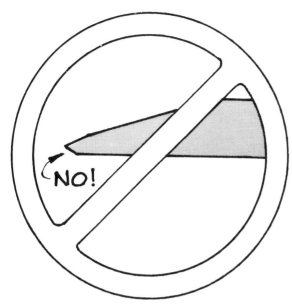

Illus. 5-2. *Any kind of bevel on the back side of the chisel will seriously reduce its cutting performance.*

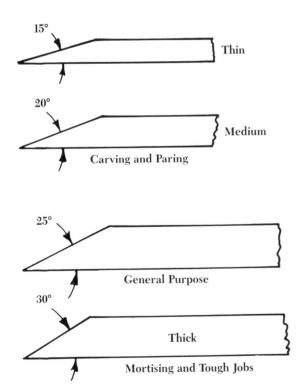

Illus. 5-3. *Typical primary bevel angles for various kinds of chisels.*

with abrasive belt machines; or 3) grinding with motorized waterstones. A hollow-ground bevel is the resulting concave-curved surface created

by the face of either a dry or wet vertical wheel grinder.

A very small *secondary (micro) bevel* is located just behind the cutting edge. (See Illus. 5-1 and 5-4.) This bevel reinforces the cutting edge, by making it stronger and reducing its tendency to chip. The secondary bevel is not created by power-grinding. It is formed by hand on a bench stone, which will be examined later.

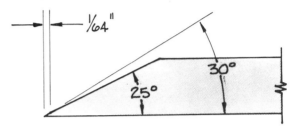

Illus. 5-4. *Recommended chisel bevel angles for general-purpose woodworking.*

Grinding should only be done when necessary. This determination is made depending upon the condition of the edge and the shape of the large, primary bevel. Illus. 5-5 depicts a dull chisel that does not need grinding. A chisel that would need

Illus. 5-5. *A dull chisel that does not need grinding. Observe the following: (1) The primary bevel is essentially unchanged and still has a flat or hollow-ground shape. (2) The dull edge reflects light. (3) The edge is still free of nicks.*

grinding is one that has nicks in its edge and a worn or used-up, convex-shaped primary bevel. (See Illus. 5-6 and 5-7.) Otherwise, skip grinding entirely and flatten and polish the back of the chisel. (See pages 56–58 for instructions on these techniques.)

Illus. 5-6. *A chisel that does need grinding to remove nicks in the edge and to restore the bevel.*

Illus. 5-8. *Scribe a square line on the back of the chisel with a scratch awl. If necessary, first color the surface with a felt-tip marker so that the scribed line will be clearly visible.*

Illus. 5-7. *The back of the chisel shown in Illus. 5-6.*

Grinding Techniques

Usually, the cutting edge should be square to the lengthwise center of the chisel, especially for butt and mortising chisels. This is not as important for paring chisels. If necessary, first grind to remove nicks and square the edge. It is helpful to scribe a line on the back of the chisel. (See Illus. 5-8–5-10.)

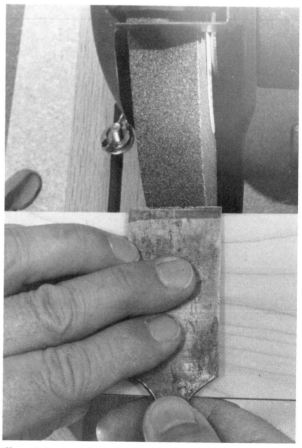

Illus. 5-9. *Grinding freehand with the bevel down to simultaneously remove the nicks and square the edge. Note the controlled grip, with the right forefinger against the tool rest.*

Illus. 5-10. *Dip the chisel frequently into water to cool it. Maintain the very same forefinger and thumb grip on the chisel.*

Grinding does not always have to be done with power tools. (See Illus. 5-11 and 5-12.) Hand-grinding with a bench abrasive stone is quicker than many think. The risks of overheating are also reduced, especially with waterstones.

Grinding can be done freehand or with various jigs or fixtures. (See Illus. 5-13–5-17.) There are many commercial devices available for both hand- and power-grinding that hold the chisel at a consistent angle. For example, a *honing guide* is used to hand-grind as well as hone on bench stones. (See Illus. 5-17–5-19.) Other guides are available for power-grinding.

Techniques for freehand and guided grinding are examined below.

Freehand Bevel-Grinding

Do not attempt freehand bevel-grinding on any power grinder that does not have a tool rest. Adjust the tool rest, if it is adjustable, to the appropriate angle. (See Illus. 5-13 and 5-14.) To

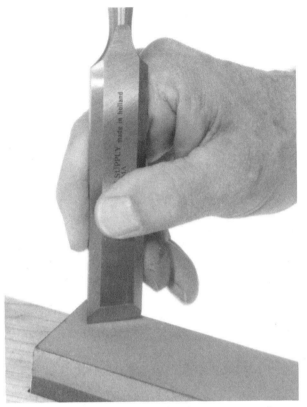

Illus. 5-11. *Hand-grinding a chisel to remove nicks while squaring the end. Apply more pressure to the side needing more material removal.*

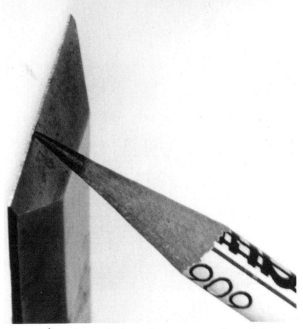

Illus. 5-12. *The nicks have been removed, and the cutting end has been ground square to its edges.*

Illus. 5-13. *Freehand-grinding a chisel on a dry grinder using its standard tool rest. Note how the forefinger under the chisel bears against the edge of the tool rest and serves as a stop. Freehand grinding on this small tool rest is difficult. It's more difficult when grinding wider tools.*

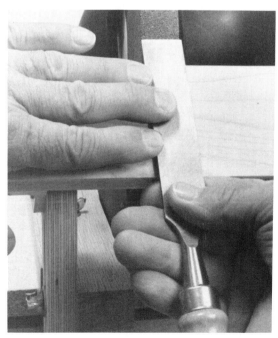

Illus. 5-14. *Freehand-grinding on a grinder with a shop-made, modified tool rest. The same technique is employed, but the larger, adjustable, tool rest makes control easier.*

hollow-grind a chisel, adjust the tool rest so that the curve of the wheel touches the mid-point of the primary bevel between the heel and the cutting edge. If grinding a flat bevel, use a motorized waterstone or an abrasive belt machine and adjust the tool rest accordingly. If hand-grinding freehand on a coarse bench stone, turn to page 55 for instructions. Use the same holding and stroking techniques as when finish-honing. Freehand bench-stone grinding and honing requires a very steady hand, good coordination, and practice. Use a honing guide when grinding.

Guided Power-Grinding

When using a grinder to grind a bevel, use an accessory jig such as shown in Illus. 5-15 and 5-16. Better grinders have heavy-duty grinding guides that fasten to or replace the standard, small tool rests.

Whenever power-grinding, use a very light touch. Concentrate so that you don't overheat

Illus. 5-15. *Controlled dry-grinding with the aid of a jig available from Highland Hardware, Atlanta, Georgia, forms a hollow-ground primary bevel.*

Illus. 5-16. *Sharpening a chisel on Makita's motorized waterstone. Note the use of the auxiliary sharpening jig used in conjunction with the machine's standard tool rest. The result will be a flat bevel.*

the edge and cool the tool frequently. Do not grind completely to form a fine, feathered edge. Stop just short so that a bit of the blunt edge remains. This will lessen the possibility of burning the edge at a very inopportune time. Complete the grinding by hand, using a honing guide on a bench stone.

Guided Hand-Grinding

Hand-grinding a tool on a bench stone with a

guide is far more effective than trying to do it freehand. (See Illus. 5-17–5-19.) Use a honing guide and an appropriate fast-cutting stone. A bevel that has been ground with a coarse stone will develop a *burr* or *wire* edge that is usually visible. (See Illus. 5-20.) A burr is the ultra-thin metal at the very edge of the tool which curls itself upward towards the back side of the blade during grinding and cannot be cut away.

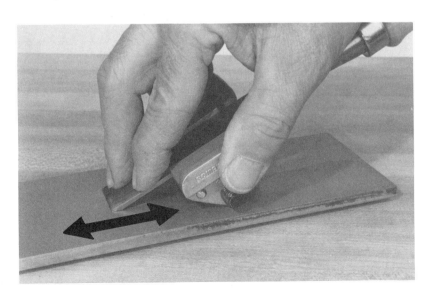

Illus. 5-17. *Hand-grinding a bevel on a coarse diamond "stone" with the aid of a honing guide. A honing guide clamps the chisel at the desired angle; its roller provides a consistent stroking motion.*

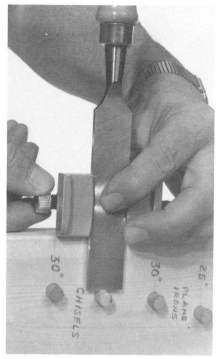

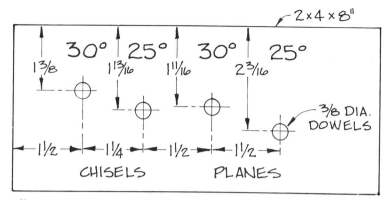

Illus. 5-18 (left). *A helpful shop-made jig for setting the amount of chisel or plane-iron projection from the honing guide to establish specific angles. The further the edge projects, the sharper the honing angle.* **Illus. 5-19 (above).** *Details for making the jig.*

Illus. 5-20. *A burr or wire edge that results from grinding the bevel.*

Flattening and Polishing the Back of Chisels

Flattening and polishing the back of chisels and similar single-bevel edge tools is an essential step which should not be done casually. (See Illus. 5-21.) This is the first step after bevel-grinding chisels or after sharpening chisels that do not require initial grinding. Often, new chisels do not have flat backs. They may be slightly twisted or warped during manufacturing. Once such corrective work is done, subsequent sharpenings for the life of the tool will be very quick and easy.

The object is to make the back of the chisel as perfectly flat and to polish it as well as is practical. The degree of edge sharpness that you eventually arrive at is directly proportional to the level of flatness and how smoothly the back is polished. Do not use vertical grinders or abrasive belts on the back of any chisel, plane iron, or similar tools.

Flatten the back with any preferable kind of bench stone or a motorized waterstone. Whatever kind of stone you use, it should be absolutely true and flat, not dished. Don't start with the coarsest abrasive. It will create unnecessarily deep scratches that will be difficult to remove later. You will be able to determine very quickly if you are making adequate progress or if you need to use a coarser grit.

If you have just ground a new bevel, begin with a few pulling or draw strokes to cut off the burr left from grinding. Clean the stone with a rag if metal particles from the burr are visible on it.

During honing, new, smaller microscopic burrs will develop and be cut away with each progressively finer honing. Illus. 5-21 shows the back of a chisel being flattened on a medium stone. Try to use the ends and corners of the stone when working the flat surfaces of chisels and plane blades (irons). Preserve the middle or center of the stone for other jobs. This routine distributes stone wear more evenly.

It is important to maintain uniform pressure

Illus. 5-21. *Flattening the back of a chisel with small circular strokes on a medium-to-fine grit stone. Working the back of the tool over the ends and corners of the stone distributes wear to the stone. The bevel is honed with long strokes, which causes the central area of the stone to wear out more.*

Illus. 5-22. *The back of this chisel needs work, to remove the deep scratches that come with the chisel directly from the manufacturer.*

Illus. 5-23. *The back of this chisel, which was flattened and honed on a soft Arkansas stone, has a sharp edge. Note the fine, visible scratches remaining. Remove these with a finer abrasive only if you want a super-sharp edge.*

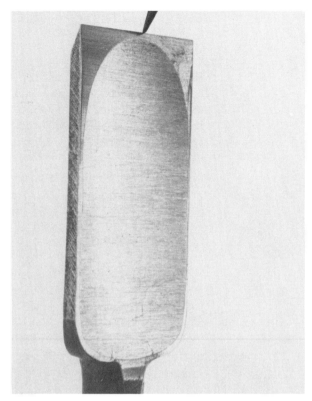

Illus. 5-24. *Note the concave shape on the back of this Japanese chisel. This design feature makes it possible to quickly and easily flatten and polish the back near the cutting edge because there is little metal that needs to be cut away.*

over the chisel as you work the surface. (See Illus. 5-21.) Use small circular strokes over the corners and ends of the stone until the back appears to be flat. (See Illus. 5-22–5-24.)

Honing

Honing is an operation done with a bench stone or motorized waterstone. This technique consists of simply using progressively finer abrasives on the back and bevel to reduce or remove the deep scratches created during grinding with coarse abrasives. The use of a honing guide for bench stone work is recommended. Once the honing guide is set and clamped to the chisel, the chisel can be flipped over. This enables you to hone the back side of the chisel after honing the bevel

side, and vice versa, always ending up with the same bevel-to-stone angle. A honing guide also retains the same angle when you change to an entirely different stone.

Honing the bevel requires much less work than honing the flat back because there's less metal to contend with. Note the design of the Japanese chisel shown in Illus. 5-24. The back of this chisel can be quickly flattened and polished near its edge, where it's most critical. Alternately honing the back and bevel will bring up another burr. (See Illus. 5-25.) Sometimes the burr is visible. At other times, you cannot see it without a magnifying glass.

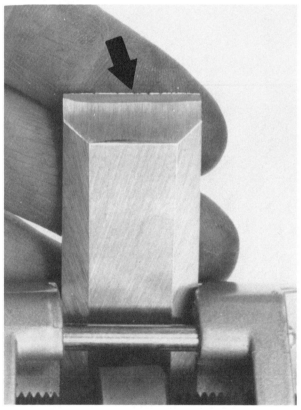

Illus. 5-25. *The burr or wire edge is clearly visible here. Sometimes you can not see it without a magnifying glass. Usually, you can feel it with the pad of your finger, as shown in Illus. 5-28.*

Once you develop a honing burr, you're almost finished. The next step is to use your finest stone to work a few strokes on the bevel and then a few on the back until the wire or burr edge is completely gone. (See Illus. 5-26.)

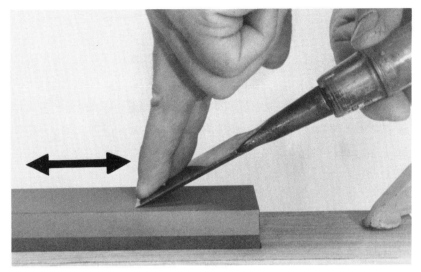

Illus. 5-26. *The techniques for freehand bevel-grinding and honing are essentially the same. Pressure is applied directly over the bevel.*

Creating the Secondary (Micro) Bevel

The secondary (micro) bevel can be created quickly with just a few strokes on your finest stone. (See Illus. 5-27.) Either adjust the honing guide a few more degrees or create the bevel freehand. The exact angle for honing to create the secondary bevel is not critical. It is a more obtuse angle that can vary from as little as 2 degrees to as much as 8 or 10 degrees. The steeper the secondary angle, the tougher the edge. The more acute the secondary angle, the more fragile the edge and the more susceptible it will be to chipping, but the easier it will make thin paring cuts.

Do not overwork the micro-bevel. Just make a few light strokes. Finally, feel the edge as shown in Illus. 5-28. If there's any indication of a burr resulting from honing the micro-bevel, remove it with a few draw or pull strokes on your finest stone.

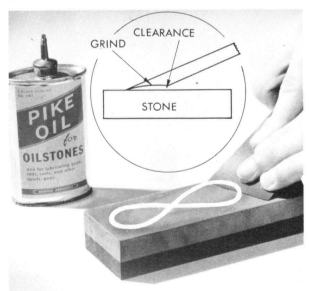

Illus. 5-27. *Traditional freehand-honing on an oilstone using a figure-eight stroke to distribute stone wear. The insert shows how to get a slight secondary bevel, by lifting the heel of the iron slightly.*

Illus. 5-28. *Feeling for a burr on the back of a sharpened chisel.*

Stropping and Polishing

Stropping and polishing give the sharpest possible edge to a cutting tool. Stropping is optional because for some jobs such as deep mortising and aggressive roughing work an edge does not need to be super-sharp. It can be done by hand on a piece of leather charged with rouge or other polishing compound. Use a draw stroke.

Power-stropping and polishing can also be accomplished with a leather or rubberized abrasive or hard-felt wheel. Do not use a soft cloth or fabric wheel to polish chisels or plane irons. These materials tend to round out the metal near the edge, creating a negative micro-bevel on the bottom or flat side of the chisel, precisely where you don't want it.

Testing the Edge

The best way to test the edge of a tool is to see how well the tool actually cuts wood. (See Illus. 5-29 and 5-30.) Test paring chisels by making cross-grain slicing cuts on the end grain of scrap pine. If the fibres are severed easily and cleanly without tearing, the chisel is very sharp. With a sharp chisel, you can produce extremely smooth cuts on any wood surface.

Maintaining a Chisel's Edge

You can maintain the sharpness of a chisel's edge for a long time by periodically stropping it. When stropping no longer works, simply create a new secondary bevel with a fine stone and strop it. You can repeat this procedure 4 to 6 times or more on flat-bevelled chisels without having to regrind them unless the edge incurs some bad nicks. Hollow-ground tools will need regrinding when, because of repeated honing, the "hollow" is no longer there or when the edge has nicks or chips.

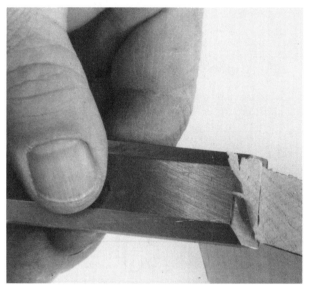

Illus. 5-29. *The ultimate test of a chisel's sharpness is to use it to pare pine end grain, as shown, to such a degree that fibres can be severed with moderate hand pressure.*

Illus. 5-30. *The end-grain surface cut with the chisel is extremely smooth, and does not have any torn fibres.*

Chapter 6

PLANE BLADES

Old-timers call the cutting blade of most common hand planes the *plane iron*. (See Illus. 6-1.) Todays plane blades are not made from iron, but of good-quality, high-carbon tool steels; these blades retain their sharp edges much longer than those that were made of iron. Blades for the entire variety of bench planes, including rabbet planes, block planes, and spokeshaves, are all sharpened in exactly the same way.

Many of the better-quality plane blades available for purchase today must have their backs flattened and edge-honed by the buyer. Few new plane or spokeshave blades are intended to be used as purchased.

Illus. 6-1. *One reliable indication that a plane iron is dull is light that is reflected off the worn cutting edge. There are minimal nicks in this edge, so the first step in sharpening would be to rework the bevel.*

Because hand-plane blades are much thinner than chisels, they are slightly more difficult to sharpen. It's extremely easy to overheat a plane blade when using the typical home-shop, high-speed dry grinder to give it a new bevel. In fact, some woodworking experts refuse to use dry power grinders on their blades at all. Instead, they just use bench stones to grind new bevels, as well as to hone. Waterstones and diamond bench stones cut fast.

Plane blades will be much easier to sharpen if you have had some experience sharpening common wood chisels. In fact, it's recommended that you completely review the chapter on sharpening wood chisels (Chapter 5) and get some actual chisel-sharpening experience before taking on plane blades (irons). Most of the techniques and procedures associated with chisel-sharpening are exactly the same as for sharpening plane blades (irons). Most will not be repeated in this chapter.

Determining the Correct Sharpening Technique

First, you must assess the condition of your blade and determine what sharpening treatments are necessary. Is it a new blade that needs to be flattened and honed, or is it well used and dull? If there are many serious nicks in the edge, then you must grind these out while simultaneously squaring the edge. (See Illus. 6-2.) This can be done in exactly the same manner as removing nicks from chisel edges. (See page 53.)

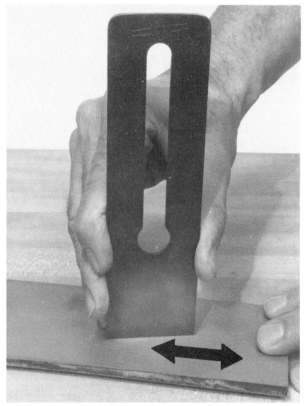

Illus. 6-2. *Hand-grinding on a diamond stone to remove nicks and to square the edge.*

There are five principal steps that must be done at some stage to single-bevel blades to make them perform to their fullest potential. These steps are: (1) grinding a bevel; (2) flattening and polishing the back; (3) honing; (4) forming the micro-bevel; and (5) stropping or polishing. Once the back is properly flattened, it should only require minimal attention for the life of the tool unless it gets rusty and pitted.

Each of these steps is described below.

Grinding the Bevel

Like a wood chisel, most plane blades can be ground to a variety of different angles. The angle chosen will be dictated by the type of wood being planed. (See Illus. 6-3.) You can grind the bevel by machine or by hand with a bench stone. The latter process is recommended over power-grinding unless you have a motorized waterstone or wet wheel grinder. (See Illus. 6-4 and 6-5.)

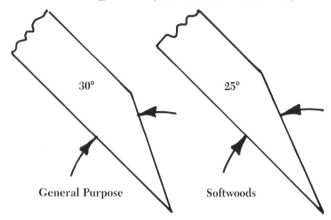

Illus. 6-3. *Left: A medium primary bevel for general use and most hardwoods. Right: A longer bevel for planing softwoods.*

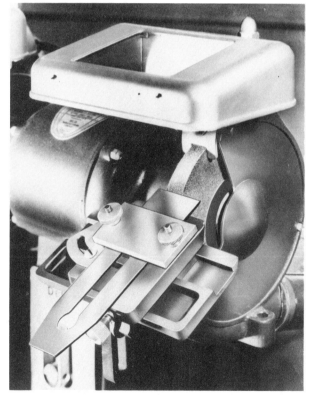

Illus. 6-4. *A new bevel can be grinded more easily with this sliding blade-grinding attachment, but a light touch and care must be used, to prevent overheating.*

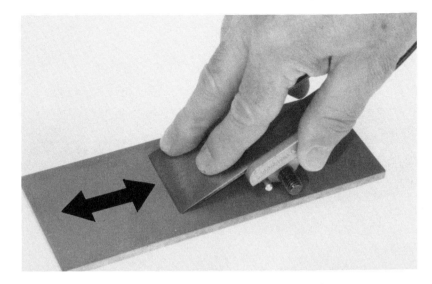

Illus. 6-5. *Hand-grinding with the aid of this honing guide on a coarse stone produces a new, perfectly flat bevel.*

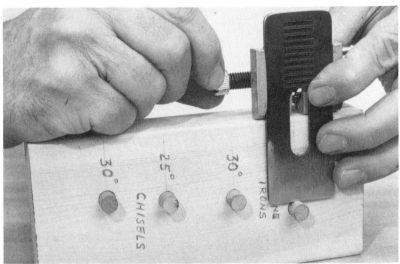

Illus. 6-6. *Setting the distance the edge of a block-plane iron projects from the jig determines the grinding (and honing) angle. This simple jig makes setting the distance easy. Details for making it are given in Illus. 5-19 on page 56.*

Hand-grinding is best done with a honing guide, to ensure that a crisp, flat primary bevel is obtained. For general-work, grind a primary bevel of 25 degrees, and later follow with a micro-bevel of 30 degrees. The jig shown in Illus. 6-6 will help you to quickly position the blade to get the desired honing and grinding angle.

The cutting edge is sometimes intentionally very slightly curved for rough planing work. (See Illus. 6-7–6-9.) Usually, however, the edge is ground perfectly straight and square. (See Illus. 6-10.) This approach is best for general work and jointing cuts such as rabbeting plane blades.

When using the honing guide, it is possible to alter the shape or squareness of the edge during

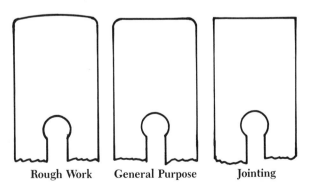

Illus. 6-7. *Typical configurations of plane-blade edges. Rabbeting and jointing plane blades are always ground with sharp, square edges.*

Illus. 6-8. *Coloring the bevel with a felt-tip marker.*

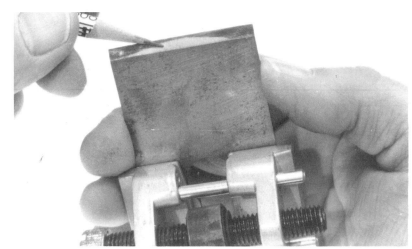

Illus. 6-9. *Inspect the colored bevel after just a few grinding strokes to determine if the angle adjustment is correct and if the edge is square.*

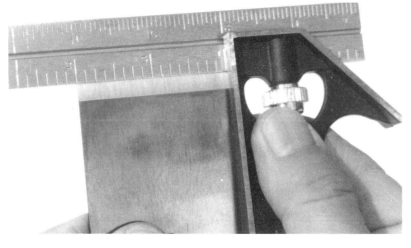

Illus. 6-10. *Checking the edge for square and straightness.*

grinding by changing the position of your pressure on the blade. Applying pressure alternately to one side and then the other will make a slightly curved cutting edge. Sharp corners are also sometimes slightly softened, as shown in Illus. 6-11. Grinding will produce a burr turned over on the back surfaces.

Flattening the Back

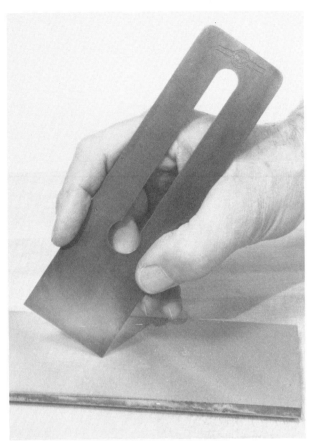

Without removing the blade from the honing guide, flip it over and remove the burr. (See Illus. 6-12.) To obtain a really sharp edge, flatten and polish the back. (See Illus. 6-13.) You must remove all the surface grinding marks left by the factory by using progressively finer abrasive grits. Ideally, you should end up with a mirror-like finish near the edge area, as shown in Illus. 6-13. Removing factory scratches from the back is the only time during the life of the tool that you will need to put so much work and effort into flattening the back. Once this has been done, all you need to do is polish the back with your finest stone during honing to keep it sharp.

Begin the major flattening process with a medium-grit diamond (320-grit) or a 600–800 grit bench waterstone. You can always use a coarser grit, if necessary. Work down to finer grits, ending with at least a 4000–6000 waterstone or another comparable stone in the 1000- to 1500-grit range. (See Illus. 6-14.)

Illus. 6-11. *Slightly rounding the corners is optional. This step is recommended only when working large surfaces such as tabletops, so plane marks show less.*

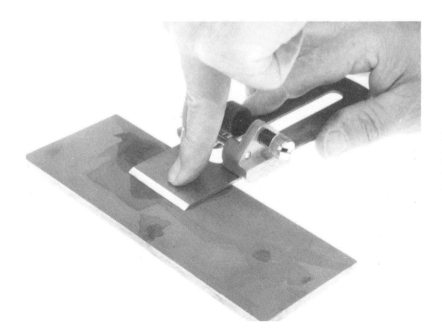

Illus. 6-12. *Flattening the back of a plane iron on a medium-grit diamond stone. The honing guide is still as originally clamped.*

Honing

With the back now flat and well-polished, flip the blade over and hone the bevel side, using the same angle as when grinding. (See Illus. 6-15.) Work progressively down through medium- and fine-grit abrasives. Honing will develop another burr, which you should remove by flipping over the blade and working it off with the back against your finest stone. Stop when there is no evidence of a remaining burr.

Forming the Micro-Bevel

The micro-bevel of a plane iron, like the micro-bevel of a chisel, toughens the primary edge of the tool. Reposition the blade in the honing guide to a steeper angle. That is, bring the blade's edge closer to the guide. If you ground the primary bevel at 25 degrees, then set the honing guide to hone the micro-bevel at about 30 degrees. Hone a micro-bevel into the primary bevel with just a few strokes on your finest stone. (See Illus. 6-15 and 6-16.) Do not overwork this

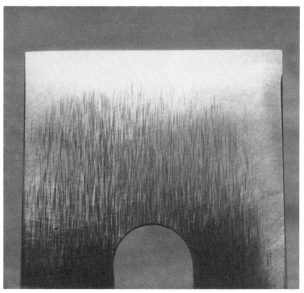

Illus. 6-13. *A close-up look at a properly flattened and polished back. Note the smooth, mirror-like finish near the cutting edge. The coarse, deep scratches indicate how rough the surface actually is as it comes from the manufacturer. Each deep scratch would be the same as a small nick in the edge if not removed.*

step; remember it is just a micro-bevel that you're trying to create. Finish with a few light strokes on the back side to remove any trace of a burr.

Illus. 6-14. *Polishing the back of a plane blade on an 8000-grit diamond stone gives a mirror-like finish.*

Illus. 6-15. *Honing with a fine waterstone. Adjust the honing guide before creating the secondary bevel.*

Illus. 6-16. *The sharpened blade. Note the small secondary (micro) bevel honed at the edge.*

Stropping and Polishing

Stropping and polishing is an optional step. Charge a leather strop with fine abrasive powder or polishing compound. Make a few pull or draw strokes on both the bevel and back sides of the blade.

Plane Iron Cap

The plane iron cap should be polished and sharpened so that the blade can function properly inside the plane. (See Illus. 6-17–6-19.) A little attention given to the plane iron cap will make your plane easier and more pleasurable to use.

Testing the Edge

Test the edge by cutting a piece of wood with the plane. (See Illus. 6-20.) You should be able to make continuous paper-thin, almost transparent shavings that hiss as they are being cut with minimal physical effort.

Maintaining the Edge

Frequent honing and stropping will keep the edge in top shape for some time before bevel-grinding again becomes necessary. The best way to maintain the edge is to sharpen it a little, more often, than to sharpen it a lot, less often.

Illus. 6-17. *Cleaning and polishing the nose of a plane iron cap with an abrasive-impregnated nylon wheel. This effort minimizes resin and pitch accumulation.*

Illus. 6-18. *Honing a perfectly flat edge on the plane iron cap so that it will fit tightly to the back surface of the plane iron.*

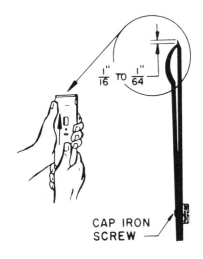

CAP IRON SCREW

Illus. 6-19 (above left). *The edge of the plane iron cap must fit tightly to the plane iron. Set it 1/16 inch from the edge for general work, closer for planing* swirling or cross-grained wood. **Illus. 6-20 (above right).** *A well-sharpened and properly adjusted plane will cut fine, paper-thin shavings.*

Chapter 7

HAND KNIVES

There are hundreds of different-shaped knives, all designed to cut wood. Some have straight, long blades. Some, such as those used for chip-carving, have short blades. Others have curved blades. All knives, from a whittler's knife to a folding pocket (jack) knife, are all sharpened in much the same way. The techniques involved in sharpening these hand knives are also essentially the same techniques used to sharpen the special carving tools and chisels examined in the next chapter. Once you learn to put a sharp edge on a knife, you'll be able to sharpen almost all wood-carving tools and other tools with a similar type of edge.

Knife-sharpening differs from chisel- and plane-blade sharpening in that the knife has two bevelled surfaces that come together to form the cutting edge. (See Illus. 7-1.) Another important difference is that hand knives are seldom struck with a mallet, as chisels can be. Consequently, a wood-carving knife can be given a thinner, more delicate edge.

The sharpness of the cutting edge of a knife is determined by the materials it is designed to cut. A handyman's utility jackknife, for example, is used to cut a variety of materials such as rope, cardboard, hardened paint, and even soft electrical wire. All such items would be hard on (or degrading to the edge of) a keenly sharpened whittler's knife.

Sharpening Angle

It is more important that you determine the best sharpening angle for your knife than the actual included cutting angles. (See Illus. 7-1.) The sharpening angle is that incline made between one side of the knife and the stone as it is applied to the stone. Obviously, the more acute the sharpening angle, the sharper the included cutting angle and the less physical force needed to slice through wood.

There are not any effective honing guides

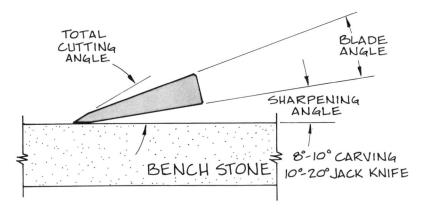

Illus. 7-1. *The basic angles involved in knife-sharpening.*

available for sharpening wood-carving knives. Carving and utility knives are best sharpened freehand on bench stones, rather than with powered grinders. Absolutely do not use dry, wheel or abrasive-belt power grinders. It is rare that a knife edge must be ground on a power grinder of any kind unless the edge is very severely nicked. Any dry-grinding is almost certain to overheat the edge, which could ruin the entire tool. For heavy material removal, use a coarse bench stone or a water-cooled machine.

Some of the basic cross-sectional shapes resulting from different approaches to sharpening a knife are shown in Illus. 7-2 and 7-3. Sharpening a carving knife is very easy. It involves these basic steps: 1) flattening the sides of the blade (sometimes optional); 2) honing the sharpening angles; 3) stropping; and 4) testing the edge.

Flattening the Sides

It is sometimes necessary to flatten the sides of the blade to make it thinner. This technique has the same function as grinding a new bevel on a chisel or plane blade. If it is not done, the small flat created by the sharpening angle (comparable

① NEW, SHARPENED KNIFE

② AFTER SUCCESSIVE SHARPENINGS

③ AFTER SAME NUMBER OF SHARPENINGS

Illus. 7-2. *The effects of many successive sharpenings.*

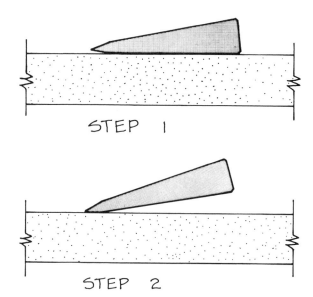

Illus. 7-3. *Above: Flattening the side. Below: Honing the sharpening angle.*

to a chisel's micro-bevel) will become too wide with repeated sharpenings. (See Illus. 7-2 and 7-3.) As the blade becomes narrower in width with use, it should also be made proportionally thinner.

It's very simple to flatten the sides of the blade or reduce blade thickness. Just apply the blade flatly to a medium-grit stone and grind it. Stroke in any direction, in circles or back and forth; just make sure that the side is flat on the stone. Flip the knife over, and do the second side. Try to work both surfaces equally.

Honing the Sharpening Angle

This is a fairly quick process. It is comparable to putting the micro-bevel on a chisel. Select a medium-to-fine-grit stone (320-United States grit, 600-grit waterstone). Lay the blade flat on the stone and tip it upward slightly to the desired angle. (See Illus. 7-4–7-6.) Work both sides equally. Make 10 to 20 continuous strokes on one side before flipping the blade over and doing the same to the opposite side. Work each side again

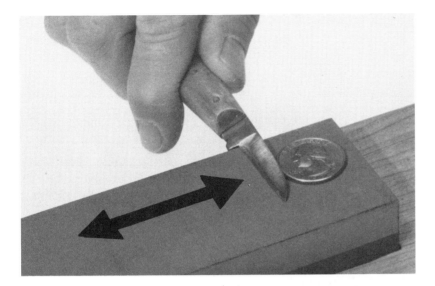

Illus. 7-4. *For a quick angle check, place a coin at the end of the stone. Make repeated back-and-forth strokes while maintaining this angle. Count the strokes made on one side before flipping the knife over to work the second side.*

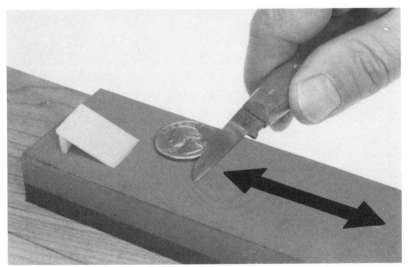

Illus. 7-5. *Working the second side of the blade. Use the same angle and the same (approximate) number of strokes. The action should be similar to that of trying to take a very thin cut off the stone.*

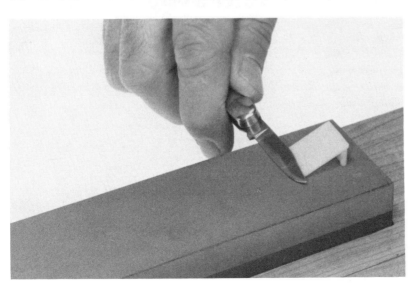

Illus. 7-6. *The pocket knife is sharpened exactly the same way, but should be given a sharpening angle of up to 25 degrees for rugged use, and an angle of 12 to 22 degrees for woodshop jobs. Shown here is a plastic guide supplied by the knife manufacturer which gives a fairly blunt 23-degree sharpening angle.*

several times until you see or can feel a burr develop. (Turn to pages 41 and 42, which show how to safely feel an edge.)

As soon as the burr is developed along the entire edge and you have honed each side with approximately the same number of strokes, stop. Go to another finer stone, or directly to stropping. Keep the same angle, and work the stone or strop to remove the burr. Flip the blade over after approximately each half-dozen strokes.

Stropping

Stropping is essential for carving knives. It takes very little time or effort to give the tool the super-sharp edge that makes it such a joy to use. Charge a leather strop with polishing compound and strop each side equally, as shown in Illus. 7-7. Power-stropping can also be accomplished

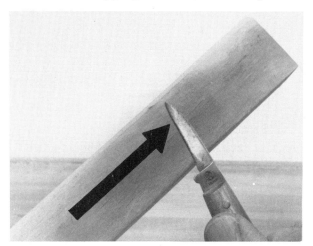

Illus. 7-7. Stropping on a composition strop charged with fine-abrasive compound. Use a draw stroke, working in one direction only. Lift the blade cleanly at the end of each stroke. Do each side uniformly.

using leather, rubberized or hard-felt wheels. Hard-felt wheels are the recommended choice.

Since much of knife sharpening must be done freehand, a slight, convex cross-sectional shape may develop on each side behind the cutting edge. This is caused by the merging of the two bevels. It does not detract from the sharpness, as long as power-stropping or polishing does not inadvertently make the cutting angle blunt. (See Illus. 7-8.)

If using soft-cotton buffers or similar polishing wheels, make sure that you do not apply the tool too aggressively into the soft surface of the wheel. This could change the micro cutting angle to a more obtuse one very quickly, and degrade the tool's performance.

Testing a Knife Edge

The best way to test a carving knife's edge is to try to slice a shaving off the end grain of a piece of pine. (See Illus. 7-9 and 7-10.) The best way to determine if the knife will cut to its ultimate sharpness is to try to slice thin shavings from a piece of foamed polystyrene plastic (Styrofoam™) without tearing or crushing the beads. (See Illus. 7-11.)

Maintaining the Edge

A few occasional strokes on each side of the blade over the leather strop should keep the edge in shape for some time before the sharpening bevel will have to be honed again.

Illus. 7-8. A sharp knife does not reflect any light anywhere along its edge.

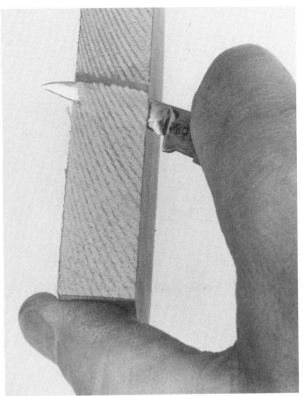

Illus. 7-9. *Test the sharpness of a carving knife by cutting a shaving from the end grain of a pine board.*

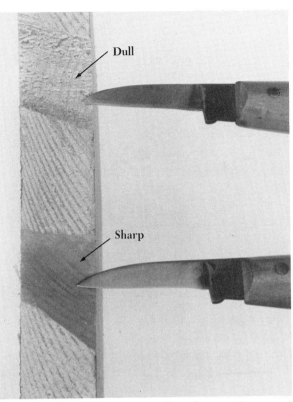

Dull

Sharp

Illus. 7-10. *Comparing the quality of cut surfaces made with a dull knife and a sharp one.*

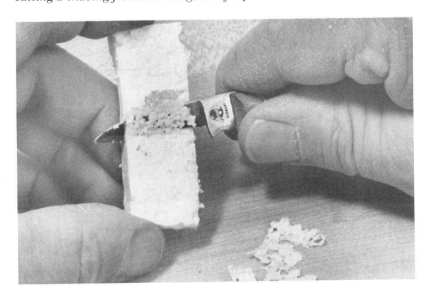

Illus. 7-11. *The ultimate indication that a knife is sharp is its ability to slice thin shavings from very soft foamed polystyrene plastic (Styrofoam®), as shown here.*

Chapter 8
CARVING TOOLS

There are hundreds of different-sized carving tools available. These tools have approximately a dozen types of edge shapes. Almost all new carving tools need to be sharpened before use. Once the tools are sharp, the professional carver will faithfully care for their edges by maintaining them intermittently during use.

For simplicity, almost all carving tools can be combined into three basic groups of similarly shaped edges, as follow: (1) tools with a straight, single edge, such as the straight or skewed chisels; (2) tools with curved, gouge-type edges (this, the biggest group, encompasses all gouges, including spoon, bent, and fishtail gouges with gradual to deep-sweep curves); and (3) V-parting and veining tools, which have two flat-edged wings joined together in the form of a "V."

Some of the very same principles employed to sharpen the chisels and carving knives explored in previous chapters apply to sharpening the many carving tools around today. Therefore, it is strongly suggested that you review the previous chapters before sharpening carving tools.

The basic principles involved in sharpening carvings tools are not difficult to learn. But because carving tools are all essentially sharpened freehand, and because the edges have a curved or V shape, they demand slightly more patience and physical coordination. The key to sharpening carving tools properly is practice. Each sharpening experience will increase your skill level, so don't be discouraged by your first results.

Bevels and Angles

A longitudinal cross section of most carving tools would appear as shown in Illus. 8-2. Carving chisels are double-bevel tools with both sides sharpened the same at approximately a 5-7 degree bevel. Gouges have slight inside bevels that are not noticeable to the casual observer. As with other tools previously covered, the secondary bevels support and strengthen the cutting edge. (Pages 75 and 76 cover how to sharpen a bevel on a gouge.)

Sharpening Chisels and Gouges

Chisels

Carving chisels are sharpened by combining some of the techniques employed to sharpen single-bevel chisels and carving knives. Essentially, carving chisels have two identical bevels, much like the design of a knife.

Illus. 8-1 and 8-2 show some very acute sharpening and honing angles used on chisels. A secondary bevel must be developed to make an included angle of at least 20 degrees. This will support and strengthen the cutting edges.

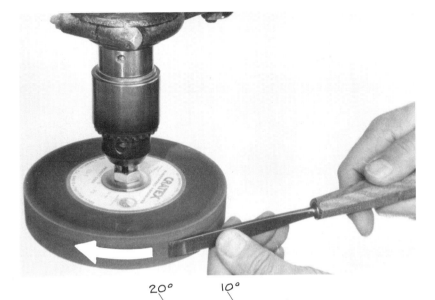

Illus. 8-1. *Honing a woodcarver's chisel on a rubberized abrasive wheel; each bevel is worked lightly and with the same number of strokes.*

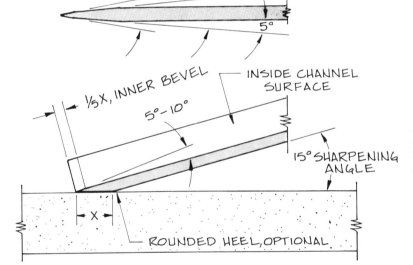

Illus. 8-2. *Lengthwise section views of carving chisels (above) and gouges (below).*

Gouges

First inspect the edge to see if light reflects off it (which will indicate that it is dull) or to determine if it is nicked. Determine what degree of sharpening the gouge needs. If necessary, grind away the nicks on a medium-grit bench stone. (See Illus. 8-3.)

Shaping the Outside Bevel. Shape the outside bevel with approximately a 15-degree sharpening angle, as shown in Illus. 8-2. Employ a long back-and-forth stroke over the length of the stone while rotating the gouge. This must be done so that the entire surface of the curved bevel is worked over the stone. Illus. 8-4–8-6 show this one-stroke progression.

Keep an eye on the edge. You may have to stroke more on some areas of the edge to shape the bevel so that it meets the curved inside edge of the channel. Developing a good outside bevel is the single most difficult technique associated with gouge-sharpening. This will take a lot of practice. If you have a motorized waterstone, this job is much easier to handle. (See Illus. 2-50 on page 40.)

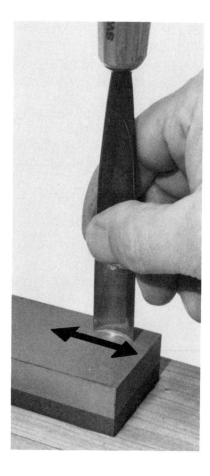

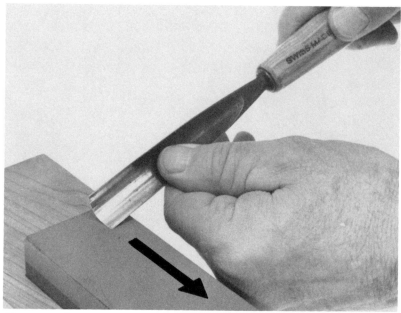

Illus. 8-3 (above left). *Grind as shown only if you have to remove nicks from the cutting edge. Use a medium-to-fine grit stone and very short strokes. Do not overgrind.* Illus. 8-4 (above right). *Starting position for the lengthwise stroke used to hone the bevel of a carving gouge.*

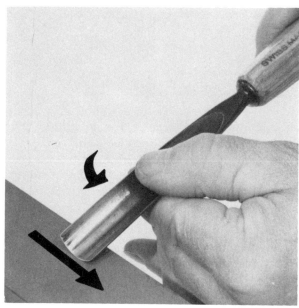

Illus. 8-5. *As the stroke continues along the stone, the gouge is simultaneously rotated in the operator's hands.*

Illus. 8-6. *The end of the stroke. Try to maintain the same bevel-to-stone angle while rotating the gouge throughout the stroke.*

Honing. This should be quick and easy. First, use a slipstone on the inside of the channel to remove the burr that resulted from shaping the bevel. (See Illus. 8-7 and 8-8.) Work a slight mini- or secondary bevel behind the cutting edge on the inside of the channel. Try to keep this minimal in width, to only about ⅛ to ¼ the length of the outside bevel. This should not be very difficult. With the channel clean, the burr removed, and the mini-bevel formed inside, you're ready to strop and/or polish.

Stropping and Polishing. Gouges can be stropped and polished by hand or power. Gouges with deep channels, however, are best stropped in their channels by hand. (See Illus. 8-9.) Gouges with narrow channels are more easily stropped on the edge of a commercial composition strop. (See Illus. 8-10.) Gouges with larger "sweeps" (curves) can be polished on a powered buffing wheel, inside and out. (See Illus. 8-11–8-13.) Otherwise, outside bevels are stropped by hand.

Testing Gouges. Test the sharpness of the gouge by making cross-grain cuts in the surface of a pine board. (See Illus. 8-14.)

Maintaining the Edge. You can keep the tool's edge extremely sharp for a long period of time by stroking the inside and outside of the gouge with a leather strop or occasionally during use by giving it a quick touch-up on a hard-felt or soft buffing wheel.

Illus. 8-7. *Using a slipstone to remove the wire edge and to hone the inside of a gouge. Hold the gouge steady while carefully stroking the stone into the channel of the gouge.*

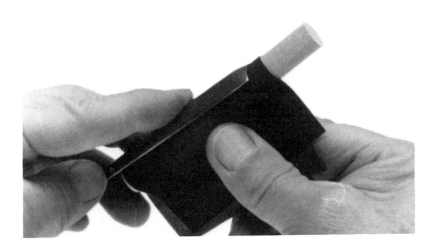

Illus. 8-8. *A fine-grit abrasive held taut over a dowel can also be used to hone the inside channel of a gouge.*

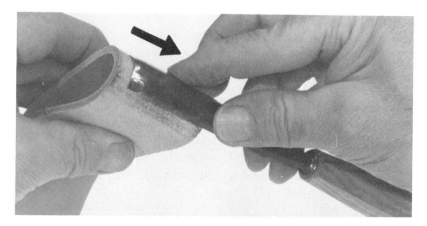

Illus. 8-9. *Stropping the inside of a gouge with a leather strop flexed to match the inside curve.*

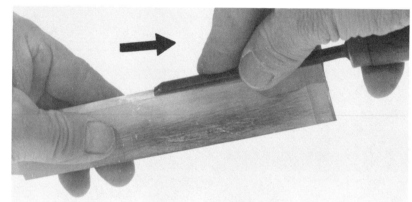

Illus. 8-10. *Stropping a small gouge on the rounding edge of a composition strop.*

Illus. 8-11 (above left). *Polishing the inside of a gouge with a soft-cloth powered buffing wheel charged with a polishing compound.* **Illus. 8-12 (above right).** *Polishing the outside bevel on a hard-felt wheel. To polish the entire bevel, the operator has to rotate the tool in his hands. Note: The wheel has to rotate away from the cutting edge.*

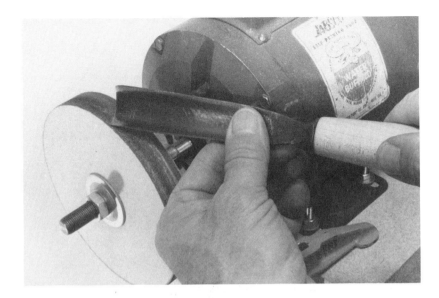

Illus. 8-13. *The operator continues to rotate the gouge, to polish the entire bevel on the hard-felt wheel.*

Illus. 8-14. *Cross-grain test cuts in pine. Left: Clean, crisp cuts made with a sharp tool. Right: Rough, torn fibres indicative of a dull tool.*

Sharpening V-Parting Tools

The V-parting tool is one of the carving tools that will present problems to the beginner when he sharpens it. However, with some commonsense and practice, you will be able to sharpen this tool without great difficulty. The V-parting tool really has three areas that have to be sharpened: the two chisel-like wings and the point area that connects them. These areas are covered below.

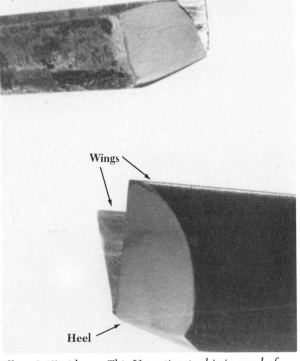

Illus. 8-15. *Above: This V-parting tool is in need of major reconditioning. Note its ragged, nicked edges and how they slant rearwards. Below: A V-parting tool that needs minor honing and polishing to give it a keen edge(s).*

Sharpening the Wings

The bevel sharpening angles are essentially the same as those for gouges. V-parting tools can also have mini-bevels on their inside channel similar to those on gouges.

When sharpening the wings, you may first have to grind the edges if they are nicked or are improperly slanted, as shown on the bottom of Illus. 8-16. You can use a wheel grinder for this, but be very careful when truing the edges. Both edges can be ground at once, making them identical. (See Illus. 8-17 and 8-18.)

Now, grind or hone the outside bevel of each wing on a bench stone at approximately a 15-degree sharpening angle. If hand-grinding, use a medium-grit bench stone. Use a fine-grit stone for honing. (See Illus. 8-19 and 8-20.) The bevels should merge exactly with the edges at the inside of the V-channel. When this is done, each wing will have a bevel. Now, you have to sharpen the point between them.

Illus. 8-17. *Truing and squaring the edges on a grinder. A very, very light touch is required, to prevent burning.*

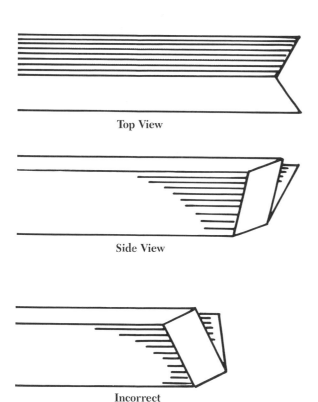

Top View

Side View

Incorrect

Illus. 8-16. *Sharpening a V-parting tool. Top: Top view. Center: Side view of a correctly sharpened V-parting tool, with its cutting edges in front of the heel. Bottom: An incorrectly sharpened V-parting tool; its heel point is ahead of the wings.*

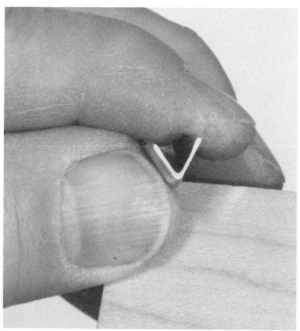

Illus. 8-18. *The edges, trued and squared.*

Illus. 8-19. *Grinding or honing one bevel of a V-parting tool. Treat each side (wing) as if it were a chisel.*

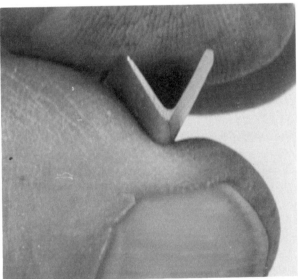

Illus. 8-20. *Stop grinding when the bevel meets the inside edge. Here one of the new bevels is completed.*

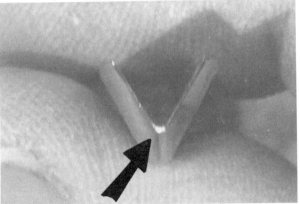

Illus. 8-21. *The intersection between the two flat bevels leaves a small area (point) that needs to be ground away.*

Sharpening the Point

Set the V-parting tool on the stone at the same (approximate) 15-degree sharpening angle used to make the wing bevels. (See Illus. 8-22.) Maintain this tool-to-stone angle while proceeding to sharpen the point as if it were a very small gouge. (See Illus. 8-22 and 8-23.) Use a short stroke while rotating the tool in your hand to grind (and/or hone) the small curved bevel about the inside point.

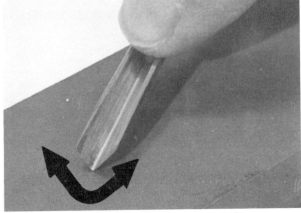

Illus. 8-22. *Work the small area between the wings as if it were a very small gouge. Note the rotating side-to-side motion.*

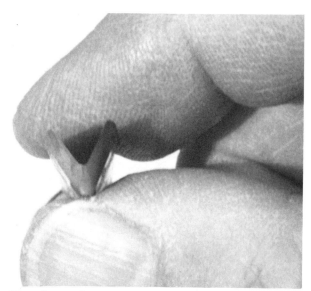

Illus. 8-23. *The V-parting tool ready to be honed with finer abrasives.*

Honing

First, make sure that you've sharpened the bevels and the point properly. To do this, look at the edge of the tool. No light should reflect from it. Also, you should be able to see or feel a wire edge along the inside of both wings. Use a slipstone to remove the burr and to cut a very small mini-bevel to the inside edges. (See Illus. 8-24.)

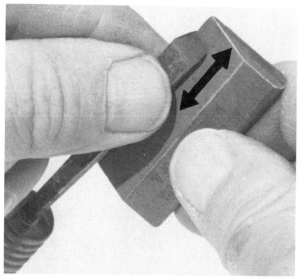

Illus. 8-24. *Using a slipstone to remove the wire edge and hone the inside.*

You may turn up another small burr on the outside. (See Illus. 8-25.) Feel for it with your finger and hone the two outside wing bevels and the small curved bevel about the point again with a fine stone.

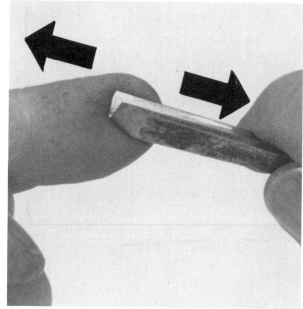

Illus. 8-25. *Feeling for a burr after honing the inside surfaces with a slipstone.*

Stropping and Polishing

Strop the outside and the inside bevels. Polishing the outside bevel on a hard-felt wheel is quick and very effective. (See Illus. 8-26 and 8-27.) It is important that this tool receive a very sharp, keen edge so that it can function to its full capabilities. A V-parting tool with an edge that is less than extremely sharp is not worth using.

Testing a V-Parting Tool

Test the sharpness of a V-parting tool by making cross-grain cuts on a block of pine. (See Illus. 8-28.) If the tool does not cut cleanly and without much physical force, it is not sharp. If an effort to rehone and restrop does not improve the cuts, then the bevels and edges should be checked.

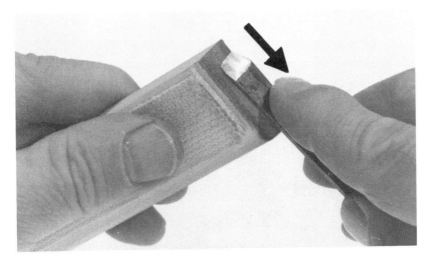

Illus. 8-26. *Stropping the inside surfaces of a V-parting tool.*

Illus. 8-28. *Making a test cut across the grain of a pine board.*

Illus. 8-27. *Rotary strops can be used to polish the outside and inside bevels of V-parting tools. Note: The strop must be rotated* away *from the cutting edge of the tool.*

Chapter 9
TURNING TOOLS

Woodturning tools, if used continuously, require more frequent sharpening than most other tools used for the same length of time. (See Illus. 9-1.) Because the wood is steadily being cut, a turning tool quickly cuts away a lot of material. This can wear out even the sharpest of edges.

Turning tools are best sharpened with power grinders, to save time and energy. Frequent sharpening is the key. Serious woodturners place their grinder nearby; some do not bother to switch it off because they sharpen so often during turning.

Shearing (Cutting) Tools

Some lathe tools are designed to slice away the wood in the form of sharply cut shavings, much like a knife peels an apple. The two tools in this category are the gouge and the skew. Both should be given very sharp edges, but excessive honing is usually a waste of time. Because these tools have an unusually heavy work load, super-sharp edges would be dulled quickly. It is more important that gouges and skews be given flat bevels that *do not* have micro or secondary bevels.

Scraping Tools

Other lathe tools are not designed to cut or slice through the wood with long, continuous shavings. Instead, when applied aggressively, these tools wear down the wood by tearing the fibres into sawdust-like waste. Sharpened scraping tools applied lightly to the turning will leave

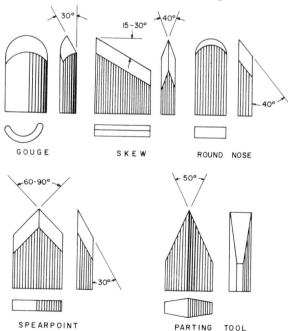

Illus. 9-1. *Cross-sections and profiles of five basic kinds of turning chisel, with their sharpening angles.*

an exceptionally fine finish on tough-to-cut end grains.

The most common scraping tools are the flat roundnose and the spearpoint. You can buy scraping tools with other special shapes, or custom-grind your own as desired.

As a rule, *do not hone* scraping turning tools after grinding them. In fact, the burr left on the edge from grinding is essential to the tool's cutting action.

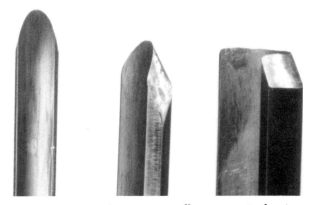

Illus. 9-2. *Left and center: Spindle gouges. Right: A roughing gouge.*

Sharpening Gouges

Gouges are slightly difficult to sharpen. Each woodturner has his own way of sharpening them. Most do work off the face of a typical dry-grinding wheel, keeping a container of water nearby in which to dip the tool. A 60- or 80-grit aluminum-oxide wheel is good for finish-grinding of all lathe tools. Seldom will you need a coarser wheel, unless you are reconditioning edges that are severely nicked, or completely re-shaping an entirely new cutting edge.

Spindle (Fingernail) and Roughing Gouges

Two basic types of gouges are spindle (fingernail) and roughing gouges. (See Illus. 9-2.) Both are sharpened in essentially the same way. Almost always, you will have to power-grind a fresh bevel when the tool dulls. Hand-grinding (or honing) with bench stones takes too much time. In fact, slow-speed wet grinders are not fast enough for professional turners. However, professionals and amateurs alike should never rush the grinding process so much that they burn the edges of their tools.

No matter how you decide to sharpen the gouge, the bevel of the gouge must be rotated through a smooth, continuous arc. Illus. 9-3–9-10 show two ways to accomplish this feat freehand. Start by adjusting your tool rest so that its surface

is horizontal and just below the center axis of the grinding wheel. Position yourself with your head (and eyes) well above the grinder, looking straight down into the face of the wheel. This will enable you to see the bevel at all times as it is rolled against the face of the wheel.

You can grind a gouge bevel with one continuous rotary motion, starting from an almost upside-down tool position. (See Illus. 9-3.) Rotate the tool, keeping the bevel against the wheel throughout the complete rolling motion.

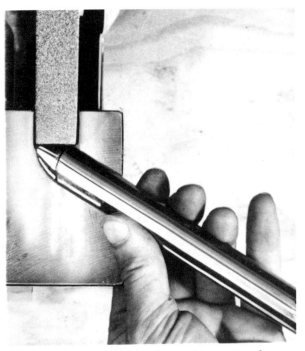

Illus. 9-3. *Starting position for making a complete roll of the gouge bevel against the face of the wheel.*

An alternate method and probably the easier one, is to make two half rolls. Grind half of the bevel with the handle to the right of the wheel. (See Illus. 9-4 and 9-5.) Grind the remaining half with the handle to the left of the wheel. (See Illus. 9-6 and 9-7.) Right-handers should keep their right hand on the handle throughout all grinding. Left-handers should simply reverse hand positions. The roughing gouge can be grinded in exactly the same way. (See Illus. 9-8–9-10.)

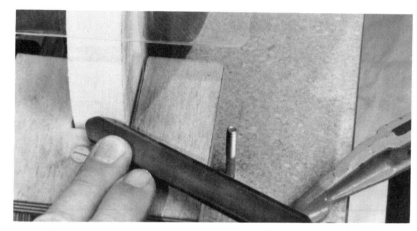

Illus. 9-4. An alternate method. This is the starting position for making a half roll from the right side. The gouge is rotated with the right hand, while the fingers on the left hand guide the gouge and touch it to the wheel.

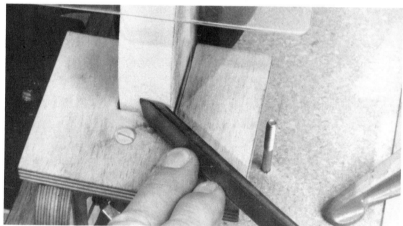

Illus. 9-5. Rotate the tool clockwise and counterclockwise, as necessary, until one half of the bevel is properly ground.

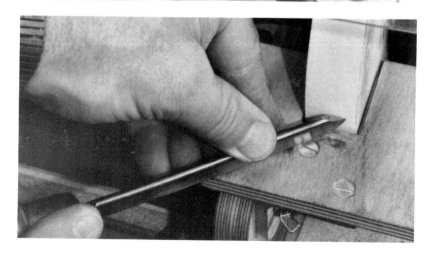

Illus. 9-6. The starting position for completing the second part of the half-roll technique. Note that the handle of the gouge is still held in the operator's right hand, and that the fingers on the left hand guide the gouge and lightly touch it against the wheel.

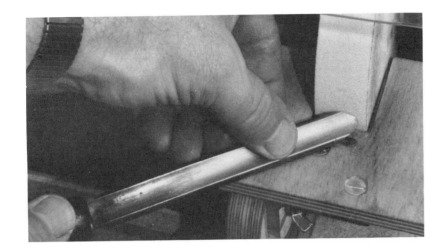

Illus. 9-7. *Rotating the tool counterclockwise to the end of the bevel completes the initial grinding.*

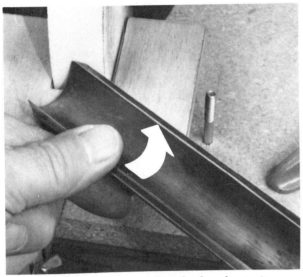

Illus. 9-8. *The starting position for bevel-grinding a roughing gouge employing the half-roll technique.*

Illus. 9-9. *Continuing the roll in a counterclockwise rotation. Note that the gouge extends to the right.*

Illus. 9-10. *This is the starting position for half-roll, bevel-grinding with the gouge extending to the left. Use a clockwise rotation.*

Honing Gouges

It is necessary to hone gouges with a medium-grit slipstone to remove the burr from the inside of the channel. (See Illus. 9-11.) When making critical finishing cuts, you will find a well-honed edge to be helpful. Hone the bevelled surface, but be careful not to round it, creating the effect of a micro-bevel. (See Illus. 9-12 and 9-13.) Generally, however, minimal effort should be devoted to honing the bevels of gouges.

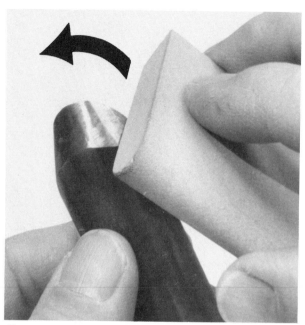

Illus. 9-13. It may be easier to hold the gouge steady and move the stone over the bevel, as shown.

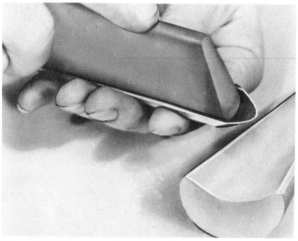

Illus. 9-11. *Using a slipstone to hone the gouge and remove the wire burr from its inside. Keep the stone flat on the inside surfaces of the channel.*

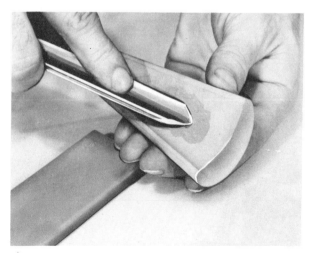

Illus. 9-12. *To get a sharp edge for making special cuts, hone the bevel; try to keep the bevel as flat as possible.*

Sharpening a Skew

It is almost always necessary to grind both bevels of the skew when the tool gets dull. (See Illus. 9-14.) The bevels must be kept as flat as possible without even a hint of any secondary bevels normally given carving tools and wood chisels. A hollow-ground skew chisel performs as well as one with a flat bevel. It is almost impossible to grind a true, hollow-ground bevel freehand on a turning skew, unless you use a guide. (See Illus. 9-15–9-17.)

Skews must be sharpened each time they become dull. Removing a micro-thin layer off each entire bevel is necessary to renew the edge. The actual sharpening angle is not as important as the flatness of the bevels. Beginners may want to use any one of the grinding aids shown in Illus. 9-15–9-17.

The big disadvantage with grinding aids or jigs is that it takes time to adjust and set up the operations. Freehand grinding is quicker, but more difficult. Beginners may want to alternate tech-

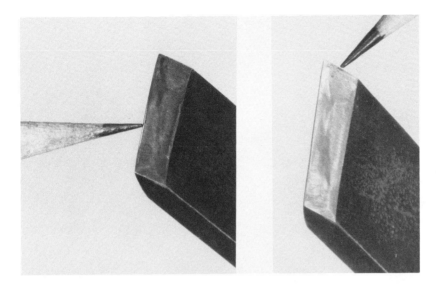

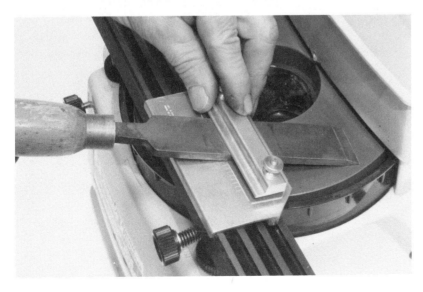

Illus. 9-14. *Two conditions on a skew that need correcting. Left: The shiny edge indicates a dull tool. Right: the rounded bevel makes the tool more difficult to control in use.*

Illus. 9-15. *Grinding one bevel of a skew using a grinding guide. The result is hollow-ground bevels. Hollow-ground bevels do not have a particular advantage or disadvantage over flat-ground bevels.*

Illus. 9-16. *Using a guide on a motorized waterstone to grind a bevel. The result is perfectly flat bevels made with quick, cool grinding.*

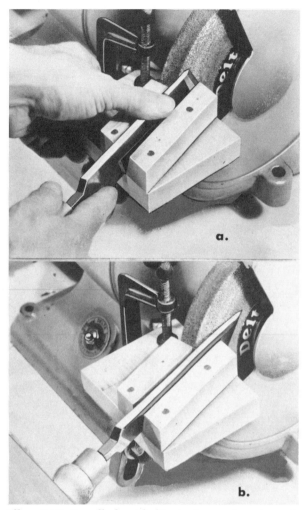

Illus. 9-17. *Bevelled guide blocks fastened to the tool rest ensure true angles for sharpening the skew. First, the skew is held against one block; then, after one side has been sharpened, it is flipped over and held against the other block.*

Illus. 9-18. *Grinding a skew bevel freehand on the side of the wheel. Use a very light touch, keeping the bevel flat against the wheel.*

Illus. 9-19. *Grinding the second bevel.*

niques. Since it's usually just a very light grinding that is necessary, freehand grinding on the side of the wheel is much easier than grinding on the face of the wheel. You can readily observe the bevel of the tool in relation to the surface of the wheel. (See Illus. 9-18 and 9-19.) When grinding on the side of the wheel, touch the skew lightly against the wheel. *Never* press it heavily against the side of the wheel. Never grind against the side of any wheel that is less than ¾ inch in thickness.

Honing a Skew

A skew is honed to remove the grinding burr, not necessarily to polish the edge. To remove the burr, just make a few strokes on a medium stone or make a pull or draw stroke away from the edge. (See Illus. 9-20.) Further honing or polishing is optional, but usually a useless effort.

Illus. 9-20. *The only really practical way to hone a skew is to make a few pull strokes on each bevel, with the cutting edge trailing over a strip of emery abrasive (or any medium stone).*

Sharpening Scraping Tools

The roundnose and the spearpoint have to be sharpened, very often, and preferably quickly. The wire edge should remain, so do not hone these tools. (See Illus. 9-21.)

Because you must sharpen these tools so frequently, you will want to sharpen them as easily and as quickly as possible. Illus. 9-22–9-24 show one technique for sharpening a flatnose, in which half of the bevel can be ground with just one sweeping motion of the tool's handle.

Sharpening a spearpoint is very easy. Simply adjust the tool rest of the grinder to the appropriate incline so that its surface approaches the wheel at approximately 30 degrees. Simply advance each edge of the spearpoint directly to the wheel. Grind only, do not remove the burrs or hone.

Sharpening Parting Tools

A parting tool is fairly easy to sharpen. You can sharpen it by supporting the tool on an inclined tool rest or by following the technique shown in Illus. 9-25. The important thing is to grind the cutting edge so that it is at the center of its blade. (See Illus. 9-26.) This tool performs much like a scraping tool, so honing is optional.

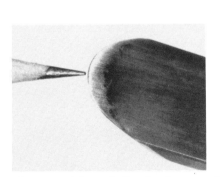

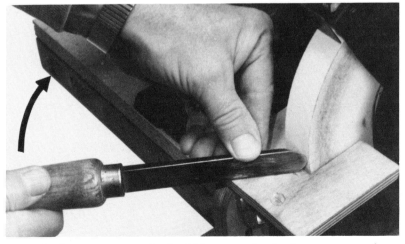

Illus. 9-21 (above left). *The flat roundnose and other scraping tools should be ground only, leaving a raised burr along the edge.* **Illus. 9-22 (above right).** *The starting position for grinding half of the bevel on a flat, roundnose scraping tool. Keep the bevel against the stone and lift the handle in one smooth sweeping motion.*

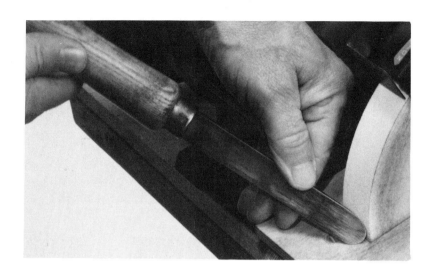

Illus. 9-23. *This position completes the grinding of one half of the roundnose bevel.*

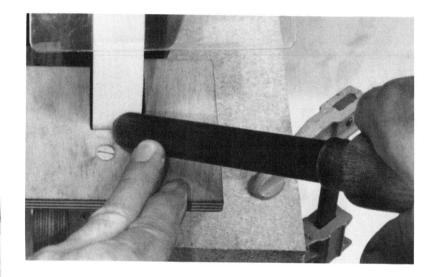

Illus. 9-24. *Grind the second half of the bevel the same way, but with the tool's handle extending to the right.*

Illus. 9-25 (above left). *One way to sharpen a parting tool. The tool support on the grinder is not adjusted to guide the tool. It could be, if desired.* **Illus. 9-26 (above right).** *Sharpening a parting tool. Shown at left is the incorrect way. The cutting edge is not at the center of the tool. Shown at right is the correct way to grind it.*

Chapter 10

DRILLING AND BORING TOOLS

Sharp drilling and boring tools are just as essential to quality workmanship as other tools. Twist drills are sharpened differently than boring tools, which usually have larger diameters. All bits with cutting spurs that sever wood fibres such as auger bits and machine spur bits are sharpened pretty much the same way. Do not oversharpen these bits; oversharpening will remove metal unnecessarily, shortening the service life of the bit. Cutters do not have to be razor-sharp.

Sharpening Twist Drills

Many woodworkers buy and use regular twist drills that are actually designed to drill metal. They use them not only to drill wood, but also to put holes in a variety of other materials. These twist drills do become dull, and their cutting edges (called a *lip*) can become chipped; when the latter happens, they don't even cut woods very well, and certainly not metal. (See Illus. 10-1.) It's also not uncommon to accidentally break off a drill bit, in which case you can either attempt to grind a new point on it or throw it away.

With a little practice, you can grind or sharpen bits so that they cut wood reasonably well. Per-

Illus. 10-1. *A dull, abused bit. Note the chipped cutting lip (edge) and the lack of clearance behind it.*

haps, they will even do a fair job of drilling metal. Metal workers demand closer tolerances to their hole diameters than is usually necessary for woodworking and general utility work.

Illus. 10-2 shows three essential requirements in twist-drill sharpening: 1) equal drill-point an-

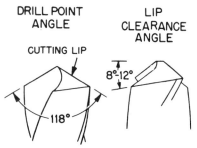

Illus. 10-2. *The geometry involved in sharpening standard twist drills.*

gles, which are usually 59 degrees each for a total angle of 118 degrees, 2) cutting lips of equal lengths, and 3) correct clearance behind the cutting lips, which is approximately 8 to 12 degrees.

A handyman's adjustable protractor can be used to check both the drill-point angle and the lengths of the cutting edge lips. (See Illus 10-3.) The appropriate clearance behind the cutting lip can be determined by visual inspection. The resulting clearance angle is not critical as long as it is approximately 8 to 12 degrees.

Clearance must be provided all along the cutting lip. Little or no clearance prevents the cutting edge from producing a chip, and the drill just will not drill. The cutting edge will be held off the work. Too much clearance weakens the cutting edge because too much metal behind the edge was removed.

Grind all twist drills without overheating them. Keep their points cool enough so that you can touch them with your bare fingers. This can be done by making very light passes over the wheel.

Freehand-Sharpening

It is fairly easy to freehand-sharpen a twist drill. Even if you do not sharpen the twist drill perfectly, it will still drill wood, although the hole may be slightly oversize. (See Illus. 10-4.) Begin by holding the bit on your forefinger, with its

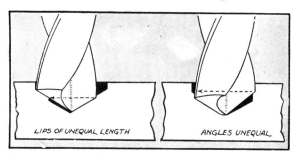

Illus. 10-4. *The effects of improper sharpening. The result is an oversized hole.*

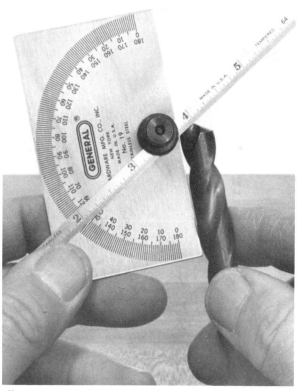

Illus. 10-3. *Checking the drill point angle and the lengths of the cutting edges (lips).*

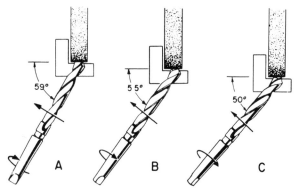

Illus. 10-5. *The three steps involved in sharpening a twist drill. Note: The operator moves the shank of the bit left and downward while simultaneously rotating it.*

SHARPENING TWIST DRILLS 95

cutting lip horizontal and the axis of the drill at
an angle of about 59 degrees. (See Illus. 10-5 and
10-6.) The actual grinding process involves three
distinct motions of the shank while the bit is held
lightly against the wheel. These three motions
are: 1) to the left; 2) in a clockwise rotation; and 3)
downward. (See Illus. 10-5.) All three are done
simultaneously. Once completed, try to do the
other side exactly the same. (See Illus. 10-7.)

Testing the Bit

Test the bit by drilling a hole in metal or plastic
and measuring its diameter. If it is equal to the
diameter of the bit, the bit is properly sharpened. (See Illus. 10-8.)

Special drill-grinding jigs that attach to grinders and self-contained, motorized drill sharpeners are commercially available. These devices
ensure perfect grinding every time. (See pages
36 and 37, which illustrate such products.)

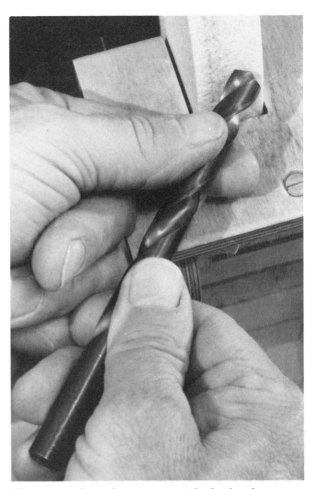

Illus. 10-7. *The ending position. The bit has been slightly rotated on its axis clockwise, and lowered slightly, and the shank has been moved to the left.*

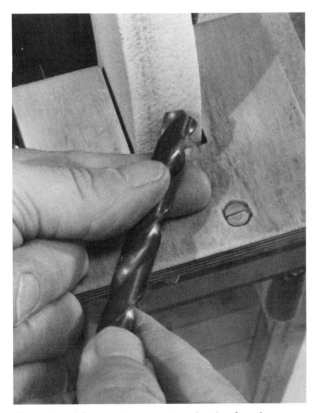

Illus. 10-6. *The starting position for freehand-sharpening a twist drill. Note that its lip is horizontal.*

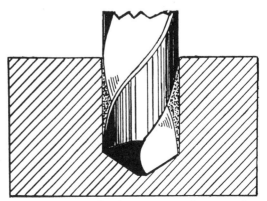

Illus. 10-8. *The result of proper grinding is a clean hole equal in diameter to the size of the drill bit.*

Sharpening Auger Bits

Auger bits are always sharpened with a smooth file. Auger bits are very easy to sharpen, and when sharp they cut extremely clean holes. There are simply two steps involved: 1) filing the lips; and 2) filing the spurs. (See Illus. 10-9.) The basic principles involved here are also used to sharpen most other hand- and power-driven bits.

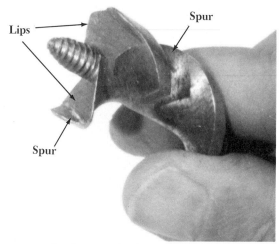

Illus. 10-9. *This bit is in bad shape. Note the shiny, nicked edges on the spurs and lips.*

Filing the Lips

Always file the cutting edge (lips) on its *upper* side only. Support or hold the bit as shown in Illus. 10-10. File both lips equally. File well back into the throat to the screw.

Filing the Spurs

Always file on the *inside* of the spur, never on the outside. (See Illus. 10-11.) Reducing the outside will impair smooth boring and change the diameter of the hole. When filing, reduce the inside face of the lip as well as the cutting edges. Try

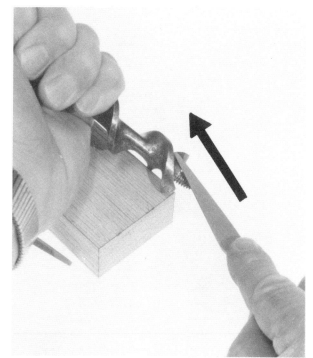

Illus. 10-10. *File the cutting edge lips on its upper surfaces only. File the lips equally.*

Illus. 10-11. *Filing the spurs.*

not to change the general shape or angle of the spur surfaces.

Auger bits are often oversharpened; when this happens, more metal is removed than necessary, thus shortening the useful life of the bit. Feel the spur edges for a burr. If one exists, gently remove it on a very fine stone. (See Illus. 10-12.) To polish and clean the screw, dip it in oil and then into fine abrasive grains; then bore into the wood. To do a superb job of filing, hone all the filed surfaces with a fine abrasive stick; this, however, is seldom necessary for most work.

Illus. 10-12. *Lightly touch the outside of the bit to an emery board to remove burrs from the spurs.*

Sharpening Multi-Spur Machine Bits

Multi-spur machine bits can be easily sharpened with a hand file. A dull bit creates many problems. (See Illus. 10-13.) It will burnish the inside walls of holes; this not only looks bad, it also makes a poor gluing surface.

Multi-spur machine bits are sharpened somewhat like auger bits. The procedure is as follows:

1. File the leading edges (face) of each spur at

approximately a 10-degree angle towards the inside. (See Illus. 10-14.)

2. File the trailing edge (back) of the spurs at a slight angle. Stroke towards the center of the tip, as shown in the insert of Illus. 10-14. Be sure to file all spurs identically so that they are the same height.

3. Sharpen the cutting lips on the up (throat) side, not on the bottom. (See Illus. 10-15.) It is important that there is a clearance of about 1/32 inch between the tips of the spurs and the cutting lips. (See Illus. 10-16.)

4. Test the bit. Attach the bit to the chuck in the drill press. Then bring the bit down into light contact with a smooth, flat board of parallel thickness, and clamp the quill. (The quill controls the feed of the drill bit into the stock.) Make sure that all the spurs are equal in height and that they will cut ahead of the cutting lip. The spurs should outline the hole, severing the fibres; the cutting lips should lift out the chips/shavings. (See Illus. 10-17.)

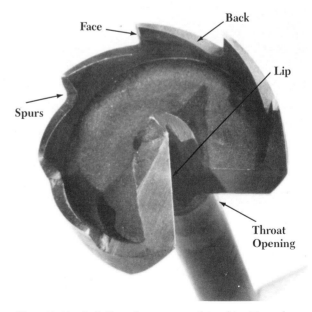

Illus. 10-13. *A dull multi-spur machine bit. Note the shiny cutting edge (lip), and the rounded, shiny points on the spurs.*

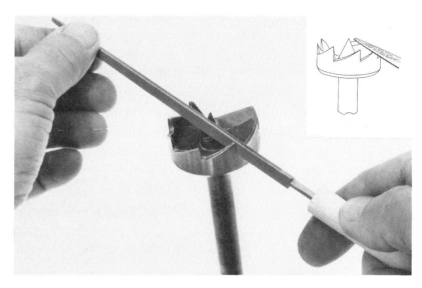

Illus. 10-14. *Sharpening the spurs on their face and on their back (insert).*

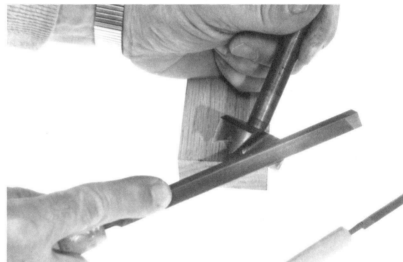

Illus. 10-15. *Filing the cutting lip, which also functions as a chip lifter.*

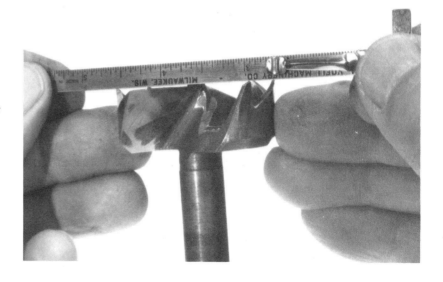

Illus. 10-16. *The points of the spurs should be about ¹⁄₃₂ inch higher than the cutting lip.*

Illus. 10-17. *A properly cutting multi-spur machine bit will outline the hole before the cutting lips cut it out.*

Sharpening Forstner Bits

In use, Forstner bits are guided by the sharp outer rim, which is bevel-ground to the inside. Unless handled carefully and used properly, these bits can be easily abused and dulled, and even destroyed. (See Illus. 10-18.) The biggest problem is that users run them at excessive rpm, which overheats, softens, and can also nick the sharp, but fragile continuous rims. To preserve the life of these bits, it is essential that you generally use them at speeds below 200 rpm and feed them slowly into the stock.

Not all Forstner bits will need a major rework like the one depicted in Illus. 10-18–10-21. Normally, Forstner bits that are properly cared for only need the following: 1) a light filing of the cutting lips as shown in Illus. 10-22 and 10-23; and 2) rim-sharpening, (i.e., honing the inside bevels of the rim with a medium- or fine-grit Arkansas slipstone, as shown in Illus. 10-24.)

Illus. 10-18. *The shiny and severely nicked edges on the rim of this Forstner bit makes it useless for quality work.*

Illus. 10-19. *Truing the edge of the rim with a file to remove nicks and to prepare it for subsequent sharpening so the entire edge of the cutting rim will contact the work's surface uniformly.*

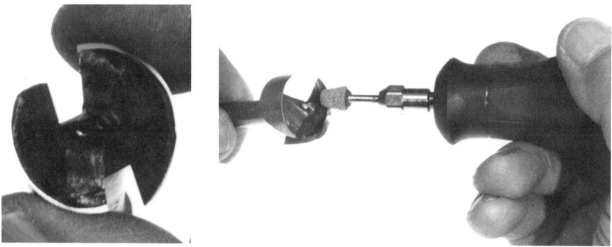

Illus. 10-20 (above left). *The trued (faced) cutting edge. Note that the shiny edge is not uniform in width.*
Illus. 10-21 (above right). *Grinding the inside rim bevel so that it matches the outside of the trued (or faced) cutting edge.*

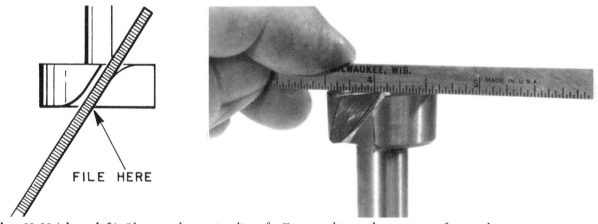

FILE HERE

Illus. 10-22 (above left). *Sharpen the cutting lips of a Forstner bit on the upper surfaces only, just as you would auger bits and multi-spur machine bits.* **Illus. 10-23 (above right).** *The edges of the two cutting lips should be 1/32 to 1/64 inch below the edges of the outside rim.*

Illus. 10-24. *Hone the inside rim bevel with a slipstone, to give it a very sharp edge. Try not to change the level or height of the rim; otherwise, the bit will wander over the surface at the beginning of the cut.*

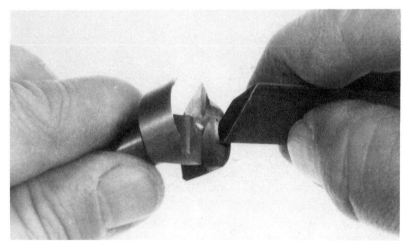

Testing a Forstner Bit

Illus. 10-25 shows and describes how to test a reconditioned or "touched-up" Forstner bit. It is recommended that all bits, but especially Forstner bits, be protected from rust. Their surfaces should also be coated with a dry spray lubricant, to minimize wall friction, heat buildup, and subsequent burnishing or actual burning of the hole walls.

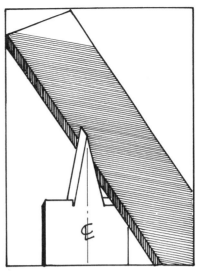

Illus. 10-26. *To sharpen a spade bit, simply file the two cutting edges (lips), maintaining the factory cutting-angles as close as possible.*

Illus. 10-25. *Testing a sharpened Forstner bit. The rim should score and sever the wood fibres in advance of the cutting lips (edges) that lift the chips out of the hole. A well-sharpened bit should have its rim contact the workpiece uniformly all around. The bit should also not wander over the surface being bored at the beginning of the cut.*

Illus. 10-27. *A correctly sharpened spade bit does not have a point that is undercut, which would weaken it.*

Sharpening Spade Bits

Spade bits can be easily sharpened. Simply pass a fine file lightly over each of the two cutters. (See Illus. 10-26.) Try to maintain the same factory-sharpened angle and to file each cutting edge equally. Maintain the taper of the point. Careless successive filings to the cutting lips could undercut the point, which would weaken it. (See Illus. 10-27.)

Sharpening Plug and Dowel Cutters

Sharpen all plug cutters on the *outside* bevel of their knife-edge rims, never on the inside of the rim. Bevel-grinding can be done freehand with a light touch on an abrasive wheel. Be very careful not to overheat and burn this thin, fine edge.

Sharpen the chip lifter with a fine file or slipstone. Do not oversharpen it. The edge of the chip lifter is sloped so that it is slightly higher towards the inside. The highest point of the chip lifter should be just slightly (about .005 inch) below the knife edge of the rim. (See Illus. 10-29.)

In general, and specifically during production use, plug cutters are often run at excessive rpm; this causes heat and resin buildup in the throat and outside surfaces. Occasional cleaning with oven cleaner and applications of dry lubrication, coupled with slower speeds, will reduce the frequency for which sharpening is required.

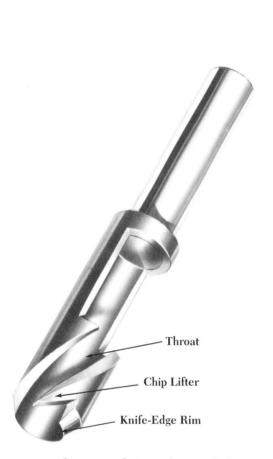

Illus. 10-28. *The essential parts of a spiral plug cutter.*

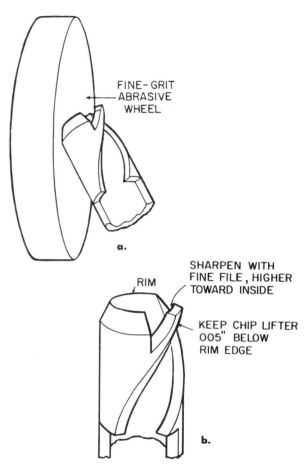

Illus. 10-29. *The details for sharpening one popular type of plug cutter.*

Chapter 11

ROUTER BITS AND SHAPER CUTTERS

Because router bits and shaper cutters rotate at very high speeds, they must remain perfectly balanced, for performance and safety reasons. (See Illus. 11-1.) Frequent and successive grinding and honing by the user can take a tool out of its rotational balance. In fact, one manufacturer has stated that router and shaper cutters, along with circular-saw blades, should only be sharpened by a professional or at the manufacturer's factory. The manufacturer further specified that router and shaper cutters should not even be honed or touched up by the home-shop woodworker.

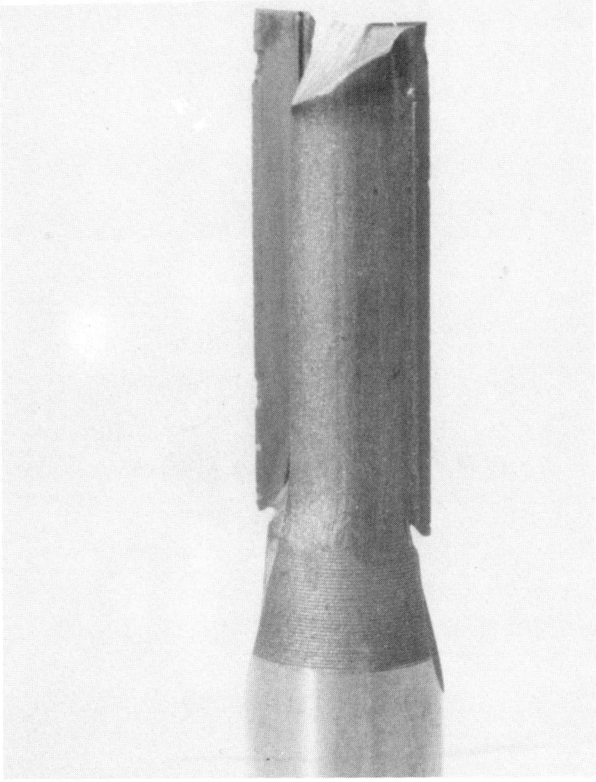

Though this position is extreme, it certainly emphasizes the importance of having router bits and shaper cutters that are properly balanced. It,

Illus. 11-1. Don't try to sharpen a nicked bit yourself. It requires major material removal that will affect its rotational balance and clearances.

Illus. 11-2. The shiny edge indicates a dull bit.

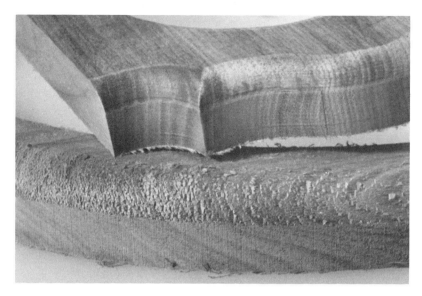

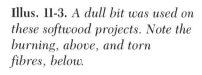

Illus. 11-3. *A dull bit was used on these softwood projects. Note the burning, above, and torn fibres, below.*

however, is not practical. If you send your bits out to a professional every time they need to be sharpened, they will be with the sharpening service more than they will be in the shop. A more practical approach is to have a professional sharpen your bits *every other time* they need sharpening, or after you have lightly touched them up with a hone several times. By following the sharpening procedures given below, you'll find that you can easily sharpen router bits and shaper cutters when you have to.

Sharpening Bits

Before sharpening a bit, clean its surfaces well; remove all gum and pitch deposits. (See Illus. 11-4 and 11-5.)

Sharpen only the inside face of the cutting edge or wing, never the outside or bevel. (See Illus. 11-6 and 11-7.) Just remember to work the surface towards the flute, and *not the bevel* behind the cutting edge. Heavier, more aggressive, material removal is regarded as grinding. Using a fine-grit abrasive to rejuvenate an edge in more of a polishing effect than a grinding one is regarded as honing.

Carbide-tipped bits can be sharpened in the home shop with diamond hones or ceramic abrasive files (sticks). It is surprising just how quickly carbide can be removed, and just how quickly an

Illus. 11-4. *Remove any resin buildup on bits before sharpening them and periodically while using them.*

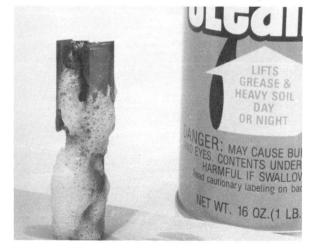

Illus. 11-5. *Cleaning a bit with oven cleaner.*

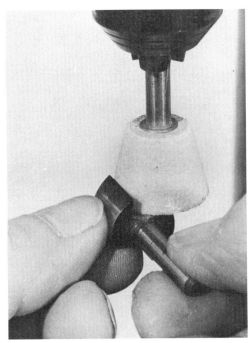

Illus. 11-6. *Very light freehand-grinding of a high-speed-steel bit using a mounted wheel in a drill press.*

Because carbide is known to be a very hard material, some people may be inclined to put more work into a touch-up honing job than is actually necessary. Examine the bit's surfaces and edge during sharpening. Keep the cutting face flat against the abrasive throughout each stroke. Stop when done.

Illus. 11-8–11-10 show sharpening technique for several different bits. The techniques are all essentially the same. Simply keep the tool flat on the abrasive and rub it back and forth. If the bit has ball-bearing pilots, remove them so that the bearing does not interfere with the sharpening strokes. (See Illus. 11-11–11-13.)

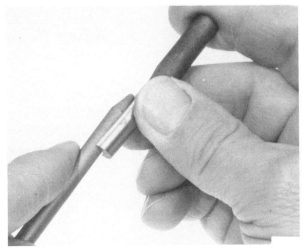

Illus. 11-8. *Honing a single-flute bit with a round diamond sharpener.*

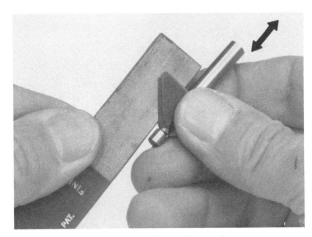

Illus. 11-7. *This high-speed-steel bit is being sharpened on a flat, abrasive diamond hone. Work only the cutting face—the surface towards the flute. Do not sharpen the bevel behind the cutting edge. Also, do not let the pilot touch the abrasive.*

edge can be reconditioned. Try to sharpen each wing or each cutting edge on the tool equally, to maintain tool balance. To ensure that the wings or cutting edge are sharpened equally, either count the sharpening strokes or alternate the cutting edges every few strokes.

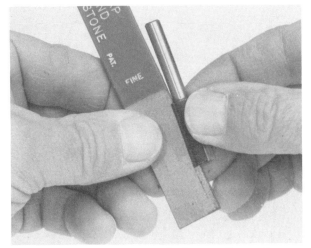

Illus. 11-9. *Touching-up a carbide-tipped straight-flute bit.*

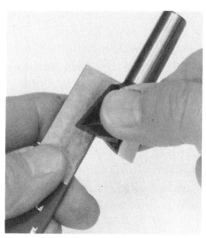

Illus. 11-10 (above left). *Dovetail bits work hard, because they always must cut to full depths in one pass. Keep them sharp, to minimize overheating and to optimize maximum performance.* **Illus. 11-11 (above right).** *If the ball-bearing pilots become jammed, remove, clean and lubricate them. If they have become damaged or worn out, replace them with new ones. Also remove them when honing.*

Illus. 11-12. *Sharpening a ball-bearing-piloted rabbet bit. Note that the bearing is removed.*

Illus. 11-13. *Large panel-raising bits are best operated at slower spindle speeds. This requires slower feeds, shallower cuts, and well-sharpened bits for good, safe work. Here a diamond paddle is being used to sharpen the wings of a big, potentially dangerous bit.*

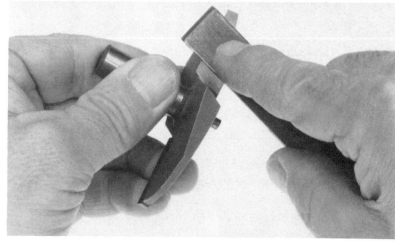

Sharpening Shaper and Moulding Head Cutters

Shaper and moulding head cutters are sharpened in essentially the same way as large router bits.

Sharpening techniques for a variety of shaper cutters are shown in Illus. 11-14–11-17.

Once you grasp the basic techniques and sharpen a few bits (or cutters), you'll quickly realize just how little time sharpening takes and how beneficial it is if done frequently. You will also realize that you can give new life to almost any rotary cutting tool by employing the techniques shown in this chapter. (See Illus. 11-18.)

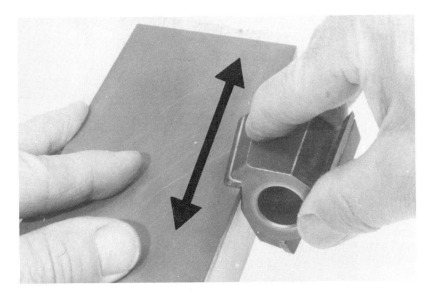

Illus. 11-15. Preliminary honing on this panel-raising bit indicates something surprising: its factory grind is not perfectly flat. This requires substantial material removal in order to sharpen the edge, and needlessly shortens the service life of the tool. The darker areas are the factory grind.

Illus. 11-14. Sharpening a three-wing, carbide-tipped panel-raising shaper cutter on a diamond abrasive stone (plate). The cutter wing is held flat on its inside face and rubbed back and forth. Do not touch any other areas or the outside bevels.

Illus. 11-16. Sharpening a solid high-speed-steel, three-wing, door-lip shaper cutter on the edge of a medium-grit aluminum oxide (India) bench stone. This technique limits the wear on the stone to its edge rather than its larger faces, which are reserved for jobs requiring larger, true, flat surfaces.

 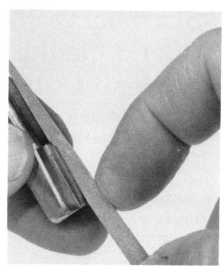

Illus. 11-17 (above left). *Using a slipstone to touch up the face surfaces of triple moulding cutters while they are still mounted in the head.* **Illus. 11-18 (above right).** *Multiple-edge carving burrs, countersink bits, and similar tools can all be easily sharpened the exact same way. Simply hone the face sides of each cutter. Here a diamond needle file is used to hone the inside faces of very small flutes.*

Chapter 12

JOINTER AND PLANER KNIVES

Every serious woodworker gains immense satisfaction from having the capabilities to sharpen and tune-up his own jointer and planer. Shutting down either of these machines to remove and sharpen the knives (blades) is perceived as a major undertaking by many woodworkers.

Keeping these tools sharp, obviously, has many benefits. Dull knives pound and burnish wood surfaces, creating problems which may not even be detected by the naked eye. Such surfaces are difficult to smooth, and they do not take glue or a finish well. Dull knives will also tear apart difficult-to-cut woods. (See Illus. 12-1 and 12-2.) Nicks in the knives create gluing problems.

There are many other reasons why knives should be properly sharpened. Two major reasons are that they make jointers and planers safer to operate, and they make woodworking enjoyable. Dull knives can simply shatter a piece of thin wood with a difficult cross-grain; this is very dangerous, wasteful, and frustrating.

Whenever possible, sharpen the knives without removing them from the cutterhead. There are several ways to do this. *Note:* Always disconnect the machine from its power source whenever sharpening or adjusting cutterhead knives. It is also a good idea to have your knives ground and balanced professionally from time to time.

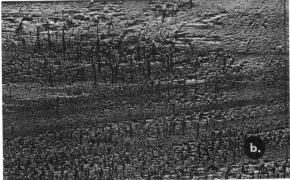
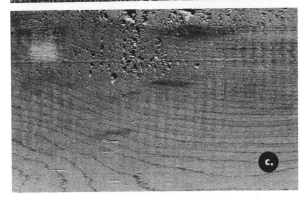

Illus. 12-1 (right). *Undesirable surface conditions traced to dull jointer or planer knives: (a) raised grain; (b) fuzzy grain; and (c) torn grain.*

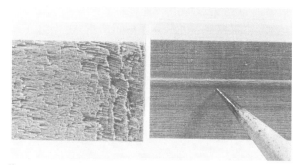

Illus. 12-2. *Very visible problems resulting from dull knives. Left: A board with cross or swirly grain. Right: A board cut by knives that have nicks. Both conditions are difficult to correct unless the knives are sharpened.*

knives in good shape between major sharpenings. Apply a few drops of honing oil to the bevels if using an oilstone.

Another quick way to hone knives in the machine is with Adwood's Planer Blade Sharpener. (See Illus. 12-6.) This tool, available from the Adwood Corp. of High Point, North Carolina, works equally well for jointer and planer knives. For safety reasons, steady the cutterhead by clamping the drive belt, as shown in Illus. 12-4.

To use the Adwood Planer Blade Sharpener, place it with the side holding the abrasive stick in the 45-degree position, so that the abrasive stone

Honing Knives in the Jointer

Honing knives while they are in the machine saves much time and energy. First, carefully clean your blades with solvent, a brush, and a rag. An easy method for honing jointer knives while they are in the cutterhead is shown in Illus. 12-3–12-5. This method is effective and can be easily and quickly done with tools you already have on hand. Use it periodically to keep the

Illus. 12-4. *Clamping the belt to the guard or to the machine stand will keep the cutterhead completely stabilized for sharpening and honing operations.*

Illus. 12-3. *Lower the in-feed table until the bevel of one knife is level and parallel to the in-feed table, as shown.*

Illus. 12-5. *A piece of paper partially covers this bench stone and protects the table surface as each knife is honed with a side-to-side motion.*

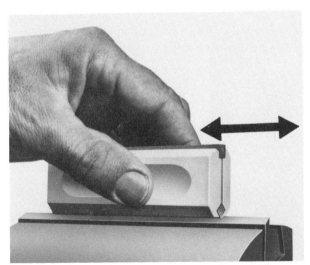

Illus. 12-6. *If you use Adwood's Plane Blade Sharpener, you can hone each knife wherever it's located.*

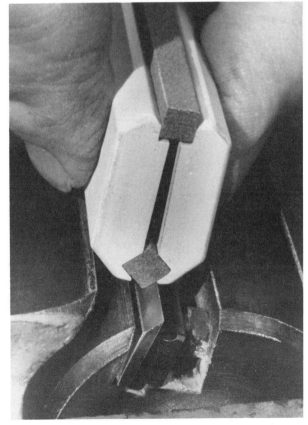

is flat on the knife bevel. (See Illus. 12-7.) Simply slide it back and forth. Count the strokes; use the same number of strokes on each knife. Do not oversharpen; this tool cuts fast. Lightly touch the face of each knife with the other stone. (See Illus. 12-8.) It is recommended that you apply honing oil to each abrasive stick before using it.

Illus. 12-7. *Sharpening the bevel side of the blade with Adwood's Plane Blade Sharpener.*

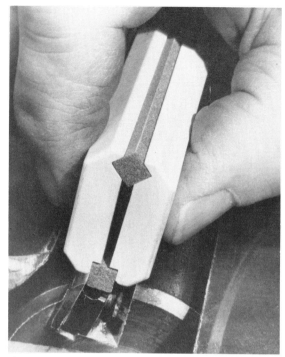

Illus. 12-8. *A light touch with the other abrasive stick in the sharpener removes the burr from the face of the knife, as shown here.*

Grinding Knives in the Jointer

When knives become nicked or their bevel has been altered because of many honings, they will need new bevels. Woodworkers have devised many different ways to grind jointer knives without removing them. One leading woodworking authority uses a mounted stone in a portable router. Routers rotate fast, and the potential for overheating the cutting edge is very high.

The electric hand drill when used in a special holder-guide works well for slower, cooler dry-grinding. Illus. 12-9–12-12 show and describe this procedure.

One key element to knife-grinding with the blades in the jointer is the need to position the knives so that each will be ground the same. This can be accomplished with a thin strip of springy wood that's part of a positioning jig. (See Illus. 12-11.) Clamp the knife-positioning jig with the end of the strip against the cutterhead, just under the knife. To get the first knife in position, coordinate the following: (1) the depth of the in-feed table; (2) the position of the cutterhead so that the knife bevel will be flat against the grinding abrasive; and (3) the lateral position of the positioning jig.

Once you are set for grinding the first knife, clamp the drive belt to stabilize the cutterhead. (See Illus. 12-4.) An alternative way to stabilize the cutterhead is to insert a wood wedge between the two ends of the cutterhead and the table.

Grind the first knife. Use the out-feed table adjustment to lower the grinder to its proper

Illus. 12-9. *You can easily grind new bevels on jointer knives without removing them when you use these drill-grinder and cutterhead indexing jigs.*

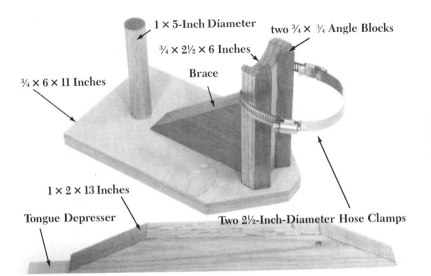

1 × 5-Inch Diameter

¾ × 2½ × 6 Inches

two ¾ × ¾ Angle Blocks

Brace

¾ × 6 × 11 Inches

1 × 2 × 13 Inches

Tongue Depresser

Two 2½-Inch-Diameter Hose Clamps

Illus. 12-10. *The general details for making the jigs for jointer-knife grinding.*

Illus. 12-11. *Grinding a jointer knife. The cutterhead is positioned with the aid of a flexible, thin wood strip which is actually part of a tongue depresser.*

Illus. 12-12. *Rotating the cutter-head rearwards to bring the next knife into position. Note that the thin wood strip flexes upward over the knife and will spring back into position under the new knife.*

height. Make a trial run with the abrasive in very light contact with the knife, to ensure that the initial grinding will not be too deep. If your out-feed table is non-adjustable, then use a system of paper shims under the shop-made grinder base, removing them one at a time to gradually lower the grinder to the knife(s). After the first knife is ground, unclamp the drive belt and rotate the cutterhead rearwards to the next knife. (See Illus. 12-11 and 12-12.)

Another setup for knife-grinding without removing blades from the jointer is shown in Illus. 12-13.

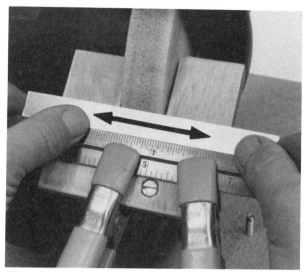

Illus. 12-14. *A guide (steel rule) is clamped to the shop-made tool rest for knife grinding.*

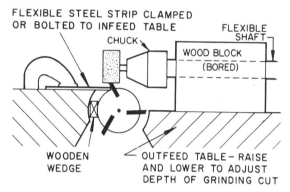

Illus. 12-13. *Another way to grind jointer knives without removing them from the machine.*

Grinding Individual Knives

Only grind individual knives that have been removed from the cutterhead when necessary, that is, to remove deep nicks or to make new bevels because other sharpening and honing operations have changed the bevels in one way or another. Here, again, there are many techniques. No matter which technique is used, each knife has to be held at the correct angle and guided smoothly as it is ground. Also, it is not only imperative that the jointer knives be ground to the predetermined angle, which is usually 35 degrees, the cutting edges must be perfectly straight. (See Illus. 12-18.) Illus. 12-14 and 12-15 show several dry-grinding methods.

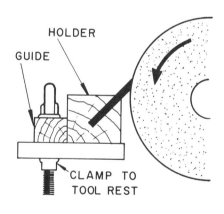

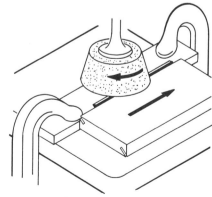

Illus. 12-15. *Other ways to grind knives individually. Top: A regular grinder is being used. Bottom: A mounted wheel in a drill press is being used.*

A motorized waterstone has many desirable features for grinding long jointer and planer knives. (See Illus. 12-16.) It can handle knives up to 16 inches in length, and has a water-cooling reservoir. Better-quality machines have a heavy-duty, self-clamping knife holder that tracks on a sturdy, milled cast-iron tool rest. (See Illus. 12-17.) The tool rest is adjustable to any angle, as well as vertically. To use the motorized waterstone efficiently, you have to practice with it and follow the instructions from the manufacturer and seller.

Illus. 12-16. *Sharpening planer knives on a Makita motorized waterstone. (Photo courtesy of Highland Hardware)*

Illus. 12-17. *A close-up look at the knife holder on a Makita motorized waterstone. The rear screws can be used to align the knife holder and adjust the amount it protrudes. Hold-down knobs clamp the blade tight against the cast-iron holder.*

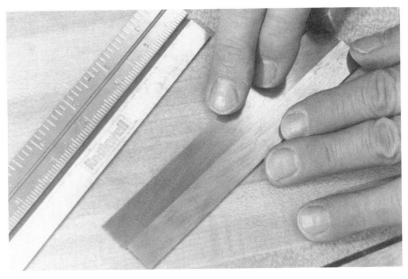

Illus. 12-18. *Check the straightness of two ground edges by comparing them to each other, as shown, or by using a true, straight edge.*

Replacing and Re-installing Knives

Replace and re-install knives into the cutterhead in accordance with the specific directions provided in the user's manual for your particular machine. It is essential that each knife project exactly the same distance from the cutterhead so each edge is in the same cutting circle. (See Illus. 12-19.) Various kinds of commercial jigs are available to assist in setting up jointer and planer knives.

Illus. 12-20 shows an easy system for re-installing jointer knives into the cutterhead. A U-shaped bar magnet or two straight bar magnets with an index mark holds the knife at a specific height projection from the cutterhead as the knife is tightened. A wooden stop block relocates the magnet each time at the exact same position for each knife.

Jointing Jointer Knives

Regardless of how carefully the knives are re-installed into the cutterhead, they are not likely to be exactly the same height in the cutting circle. If one knife projects just slightly more than

Illus. 12-19. How the jointer functions. CB is the cutting bevel ground on the knife. CA is the cutting angle of the knife.

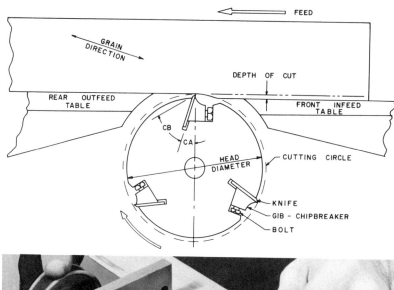

Illus. 12-20. The knives are being set back into the cutterhead with the aid of a magnet, to ensure that each knife projects to exactly the same height.

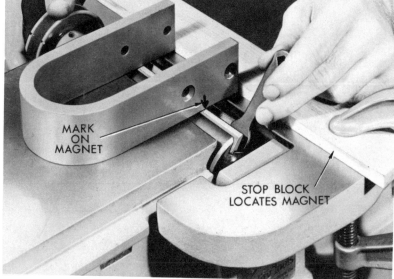

the others, it will work much harder. It will dull quicker, and the finished cut surface will not be as flat, smooth, or true as it can be.

Jointing makes every knife cut equally, so the work load is shared uniformly by all the knives. Jointing also has the added benefit of giving strength to the cutting edge.

To bring all knife edges into the same cutting circle, touch them very, very lightly with an abrasive stone. (See Illus. 12-21.) Clamp a board to the in-feed table; this board will act as a stop. Place the stone on the out-feed table on a piece of paper. Slowly lower the in-feed table until the stone just barely touches the knives. There should be very few sparks visible, just a hissing sound.

Move the stone over the full length of the knives. Stop the machine and examine the edges to be sure that all edges have been touched. They should show only a hairline mark at the tip of each knife. Ideally, the first jointing of freshly sharpened knives will produce micro-secondary bevels that will be under ⅟₆₄ inch in width.

Note: Be very careful when jointing knives. Wear full face and eye protection. Stand away from the rotation (to the out-feed side of the table) and make sure that you are not wearing loose clothing or jewelry. The operation can be performed several times between knife grindings. (See Illus. 12-22.) When the bevel created by the knife-jointing operation becomes about ⅟₃₂ inch in width, the knives must be reground.

Honing

Honing is done periodically between jointing, and only immediately after jointing if a super-sharp edge is desired. Illus. 12-5 shows a honing operation.

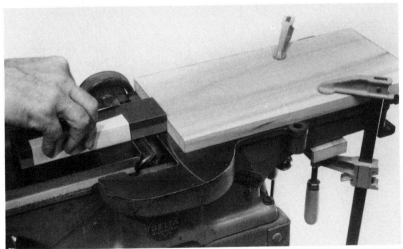
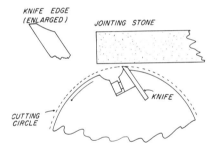

Illus. 12-21 (above left). *When jointer knives are "jointed," all of their edges are brought into the same cutting circle (height). To do this, very lightly touch an abrasive stone to the knife edges while the cutterhead is rotating under power.* **Illus. 12-22 (above right).** *The knife-jointing operation puts a small, secondary micro-bevel, just a hairline in width, on the knife edge.*

Chapter 13
SCREWDRIVERS, SCRAPERS, AND SAWS

Sharpening Screwdrivers

With use, standard slotted and Phillips screwdrivers often need to be "dressed" or sharpened. A slotted screwdriver is often used for many jobs other than driving screws. It can be used to pry open items, to chisel, and to scrape. Because it is used for so many jobs, its edges and blade wear to a point where it is no longer effective for driving screws. (See Illus. 13-1 and 13-2.)

A screwdriver is sharpened as follows: First, if necessary, dress the sides to that the blade is symmetrical in shape across its width. (See Illus. 13-3.) Next, square the end. (See Illus. 13-4.) A square end is important. Check the end with a square. (See Illus. 13-5.) Finally, grind the blade

to the appropriate thickness to fit the screw slot. (See Illus. 13-6.) In this operation, hold the blade high on the circumference of the wheel. Try to

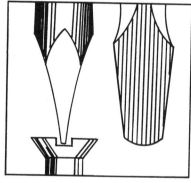

Illus. 13-2. *A screwdriver needs sharpening when its tip is too thin or when the blade is rounded.*

Illus. 13-1. *Worn and abused screwdriver blades are not in proper condition for driving screws.*

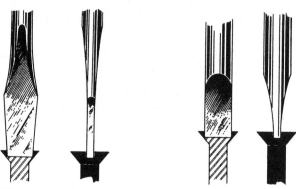

Illus. 13-3. *Shapes of screwdrivers when properly sharpened. Left: Front and side views of a common screwdriver. Right: Front and side views of an electrician's or cabinet screwdriver.*

Illus. 13-4. *Grinding an end square.*

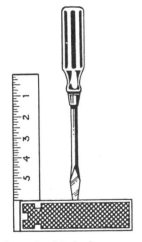

Illus. 13-5. *Checking the blade for squareness.*

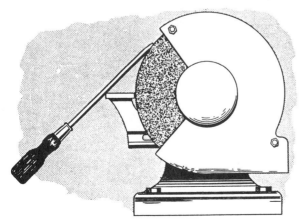

Illus. 13-6. *Grinding the blade to the appropriate thickness. Make the faces parallel or nearly parallel.*

make the two faces parallel or nearly parallel. A properly ground screwdriver will not have the tendency to climb out of the screw slot when being turned.

Worn Phillips screwdrivers can be touched up on a bench stone. (See Illus. 13-7.) Use a square-cornered slipstone to clean up the flutes.

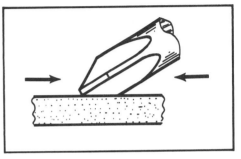

Illus. 13-7. *Sharpening a Phillips screwdriver on a bench stone. Use a square-cornered slipstone to clean up the flutes.*

Sharpening Scrapers

Hand Scrapers

You will have to dress, hone, and burnish a new or dull scraper to form and turn a burr that does the cutting. By practising the basic steps involved, you will soon be able to produce a suitable scraper edge that's a joy to use. (See Illus. 13-9 and 13-10.)

First, dress the long edges of the scraper with a single-cut file, to produce a true, square edge. (See Illus. 13-11.) Next, hone the edge on a stone. Hold the scraper slightly diagonally as you move it over the stone so that you don't wear a groove into the surface of the stone. (See Illus. 13-12.) Hone the flat sides very lightly. (See Illus. 13-13.) This will remove honing burrs.

Next burnish the edge. (See Illus. 13-14 and 13-15.) Start at 90 degrees; make several firm strokes to create a burr. Then gradually incline the burnisher with several multiple passes with fairly light pressure until it is about 15 degrees off horizontal or 85 degrees to the face of the

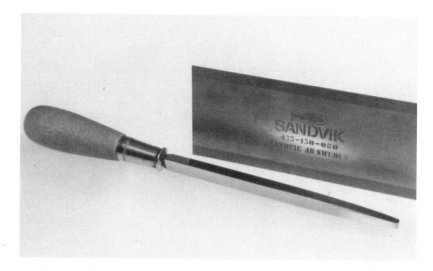

Illus. 13-8. *A scraper and a hardened triangular burnisher.*

Illus. 13-9. *A sharp scraper cuts very thin shavings with its burr edges.*

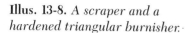

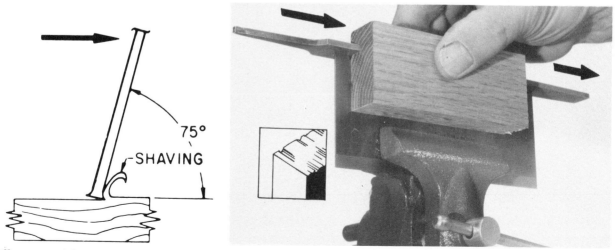

Illus. 13-10 (above left). *The cutting action of a scraper.* **Illus. 13-11 (above right).** *With the scraper held vertically in a vise, file the edge to square it and to remove nicks. Use a single-cut mill file in a slotted hardwood block, as shown, to make a perfectly square edge.*

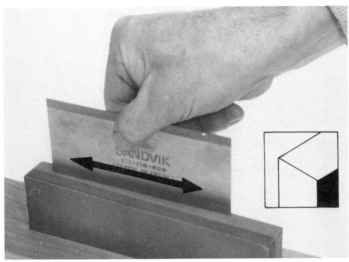

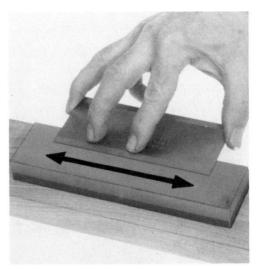

Illus. 13-12 (above left). *Hone the edge of the scraper on a fine-grit stone. The edge of the stone is used because the scraper may scratch or wear the surface.* **Illus. 13-13 (above right).** *Hone the faces lightly to remove any burrs.*

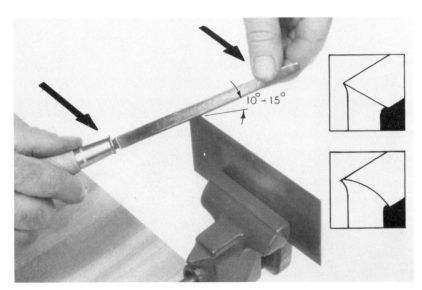

Illus. 13-14. *Burnishing forms the cutting burr(s). Apply a few drops of oil to the burnisher. Then draw it over the edge in multiple strokes, gradually increasing the angle of the burnisher to not more than 15 degrees, as shown.*

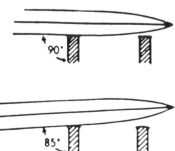

Illus. 13-15. *Burnishing steps. Above: When you apply firm pressure to a flat edge, you will form a burr. Below: The burr being formed and turned to make a hooked edge.*

blade. Do not exert too much pressure on the burnisher when turning the burr.

When the burr of the scraper dulls, you can bring it back again several times before the edge must be redressed and honed. (See Illus. 13-16.)

Sharpening Curved Scrapers

Curved scrapers are sharpened in essentially the same way as hand scrapers. (See Illus. 13-17.) Hone their edges with slipstones and turn the burr of concave edges with a round burnisher. (See Illus. 13-18.)

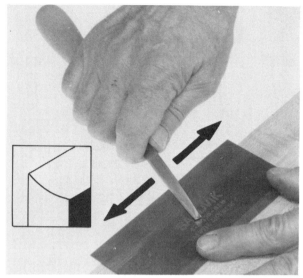

Illus. 13-16. *Resharpening without rehoning is possible. Three to four strokes, as shown, will flatten the existing burr. Then reburnish to turn the burr as before.*

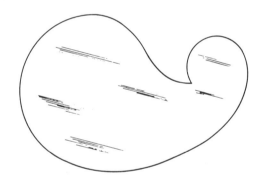

Illus. 13-17. *A swan-neck scraper.*

Illus. 13-18. *A round burnisher.*

Sharpening Saws

This section on sharpening saws deals only with light touch-up filing, not the major processes involved in regrinding, jointing, gumming, and setting hand and power saws. There are hundreds of different kinds of saws and saw blades available today, including handsaws (Western and Japanese styles), power circular blades, new, thin kerf saws, band-saw and scroll-saw blades, chain saws, pruning saws, etc. All cut wood, but all are different in their design and cutting actions. The equipment needed to sharpen saws properly is expensive, and this is simply not a practical expectation for the home workshop.

Filing Handsaws

Handsaws can be filed by hand several times before they need rework by a professional. Handsaw filing techniques have really not changed in the last hundred years. The following sections explore sharpening techniques for crosscut and rip handsaws.

Crosscut Saw.   The teeth on a crosscut saw are of identical, sharp knife-like points arranged to sever the fibres of the wood across the grain. (See Illus. 13-19.) To sharpen a crosscut saw, mount it

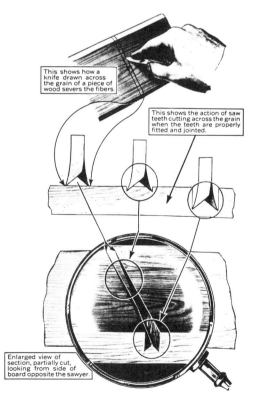

Illus. 13-19. *The cutting action of a properly filed and set crosscut saw.*

in a vise or filing clamp with the saw handle to the right. (See Illus. 13-20, top.) Before filing the teeth bevels, pass a fine, flat file very lightly over the tops or along the "line" of teeth to make a "shiner," or bright top. (See Illus. 13-21.) This is

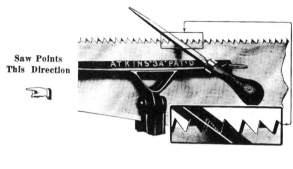

Saw Points
This Direction

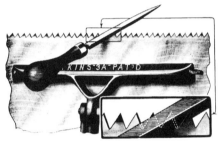

Saw Points
This Direction

Illus. 13-20. *Filing handsaws.*

known as *jointing*, and it is used as a guide to filing each tooth. Use a 6- or 7-inch slim-taper, three-square (triangular) file to joint. Start in the gullet to the *left* of the first tooth. (See Illus. 13-20, top.) Hold the file so as to maintain the existing angle. Push it across the saw, bringing each tooth to a point; leave just a little of the "shiner" on the tooth to the right of your file. Duplicate this procedure in every other gullet, progressing to the handle of the saw.

Reverse the saw. (See Illus. 13-20, bottom.) Place the saw handle so that it is now to your left. Proceed in exactly the same manner as previously, except start in the gullet to the *right* of the first tooth set away from you. File each tooth to a sharp point.

Rip Saws. A rip saw is used to cut along the grain of wood. It is sharpened exactly like a crosscut saw, except there is no bevel to the tooth of a rip saw. (See Illus. 13-22 and 13-23.) Stroke the file straight across the tooth at right angles to the blade. There are no bevels. Rip saws have chisel-like edges, not knife points.

Shape of cross-cut saw teeth

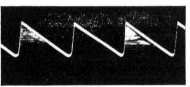

Shape of rip saw teeth

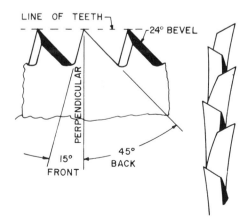

Illus. 13-21. *An enlarged view of crosscut teeth.*

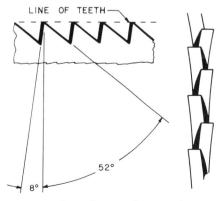

Illus. 13-22. *An enlarged view of rip teeth. Note the chisel-like cutting edges, and how they differ from the pointed crosscut teeth.*

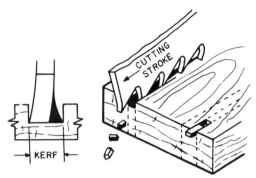

Illus. 13-23. *Left: The cross section of rip teeth. Right: The cutting action of a rip saw.*

Techniques for Sharpening Handsaws

Choose as long a file as possible. A long file will make smoother, steadier, and more uniform strokes. Always try to maintain the original shape of the teeth. File all gullets to uniform depths.

Your saw will not need setting every time you sharpen it, but it is a good idea to joint it lightly before each filing. When the saw does drag or pinch in the kerfs, it will need setting. This is because the teeth are not cutting a kerf wide enough for blade clearance.

Dull scroll-saw blades, coping-saw blades, and some band-saw blades can also be sharpened with the procedures just described. In fact, hand-filing with a very small file will actually improve the performance of new blades, as well as rejuvenate dull ones.

Sharpening Circular-Saw Blades

Approximately 90 percent of all circular-saw blades used today have carbide-tipped teeth. These teeth spread wear over a hard and durable blade body. So, unless abused, a sharp, well-maintained carbide-tipped blade should cut well for a very long period of time before it has to be sharpened.

Do *not* attempt to touch-file carbide teeth with diamond or ceramic files or hones. You can ruin a carbide tooth easily by attempting to file or hone it yourself. Unlike steel blades with teeth that are bent for kerf clearance, a carbide-tooth blade has back-and-side-bevel tooth clearances that are ground to precise and extremely important angles. Some of these critical angles have a radial clearance of as little as 1½ degrees; other clearances are just 3 and 5 degrees.

Attempting to duplicate such angles by hand is impossible. It is certain to cause problems that can only be corrected (if still possible) with a major regrind. This wastes away the blade, because it removes more material from the blade than would normally be removed if done regularly by a competent sharpening service.

There are three things you can do to prolong the life of all saw blades, but especially carbide-tipped circular-saw blades. They are as follows:

1. Clean them regularly. (See Illus. 13-24.) Dirty, pitch-loaded blades do not cut efficiently and will become dull prematurely.

Illus. 13-24. *Keeping a blade clean of gum or pitch deposits adds life to the blade and ensures that it will cut at its maximum efficiency.*

2. Resharpen the blade before it actually gets dull. Dull blades quickly generate friction and heat, which will increase when the blade is used. If you use a dull blade, you will eventually have to grind away more material to regain the original tooth form and clearance. This practice is wasteful.

A good carbide blade can be reground as many as 25 times, depending upon the care and attention it is given and the original thickness of the carbide tips.

3. Coat the blades with protective spray-on dry lubricant. Periodical treatments will inhibit resin buildup and reduce surface friction.

Steel Circular-Saw Blades

The home woodworker can maintain the edge sharpness of steel circular-saw blades by touching them up with a file. First, touch up the teeth lightly with a file several times; then send the blade to a professional sharpening service to be reconditioned or sharpened.

To touch up a steel circular-saw blade, do the following:

1. Joint the teeth. Install the saw blade rearwards in the table saw. Make sure that the power is disconnected when doing this. Lower the blade until it projects ¹⁄₆₄ to ¹⁄₃₂ inch above the table. Check the projection. Start the saw, and lightly move an abrasive stone over the blade. It should only slightly touch each tooth. This will make the blade perfectly round, and also produce "shiners" on each tooth.

2. Either remove the blade or unplug the saw and file the blade while it is still mounted to the saw arbor. (See Illus. 13-25 and 13-26.)

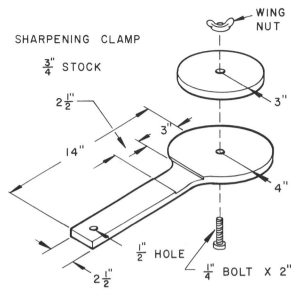

Illus. 13-26. *Details for making a circular-saw blade clamp for touch-up filing.*

3. File each tooth bevel as uniformly as possible with a fine file. Hold and stroke the file so as to maintain the existing bevel angles. (See Illus. 13-27.)

4. File each tooth; use two or three firm strokes to remove the flat (shiner) caused by jointing.

5. Re-install the blade correctly and test it.

Illus. 13-25. *Touch-up filing of a steel blade. Do not attempt this with a carbide-tipped blade.*

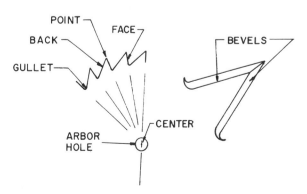

Illus. 13-27. *Parts of a typical saw tooth on a steel blade.*

GLOSSARY

Abrasive   Any material of natural or man-made origin used to grind or polish metal.

Arbor   The rotating shaft of a motor or a mandrel onto which an abrasive is mounted.

Back   The side of a blade or cutting tooth that *does not* come into direct contact with a shaving or chip.

Bevel   The inclined surface that is sharpened on a chisel, plane blade, or knife blade.

Bevel Angle   The result of grinding an incline, measured in degrees, from the face of a knife or cutter to the flat or straight back to form a sharp cutting edge.

Burnish   To polish or to form a burr edge on a hard tool by rubbing it with another hard tool.

Burr   (also known as the *wire edge* or *feathered edge*.) The small curled metal remaining on a freshly sharpened tool edge after grinding.

Burr (Tool)   A small rotary file.

Carbide Tip   A small piece of tungsten carbide soldered to a steel blade or cutter that is sharpened to be the cutting edge.

Chuck   Part of a hand drill or drill press that grips the bit on a cutter.

Clearance   A space directly behind a tool's cutting edge that is created when a bevel is ground or a tooth is bent. This space eliminates friction in a cut.

Clearance Angle   The amount of bevel on the back or side of a cutter, designated in degrees.

Concave   An inward curve or surface.

Convex   An outward curve or surface.

Cutting Angle   (also known as "rake," "hook," or "chip angle" on power-driven cutters). The measured angle between a line perpendicular to the surface being cut and the face side of the tooth or knife.

Cutting Circle   The path made by the edge or edges of rotating knives or blades.

Dress   To improve or condition the surface of a grinding wheel or other tool.

Dresser   A tool that wears down abrasive stones or wheels to make their surfaces flat and true or of another specific shape.

Edge   The sharp, pointed cutting part of a blade or tool.

Face   The front or forward side of a cutting tooth or blade which contacts the chip or shaving as it is cut.

Feed Speed   The rate at which a tool or material is advanced during the cutting process. The feed speed is usually designated by inches or feet per minute.

Flute   The channel-like straight or spiral groove of a bit or cutter that removes the chips from a hole or a cut.

Glazed   To become glossy or smooth, or a worn abrasive filled with metal particles.

Grind   Coarse wearing away of a softer material by the abrasive action of a harder material.

Grinder   Any power-driven abrasive tool.

Grit   A classification that describes the size of abrasive granules (or grains). Abrasive granules are sized according to a grit numbering system.

Gullet   The opening or pocket in front of a saw tooth or cutter that deflects and carries chips away from and out of the cut.

Hollow Grind   A tool bevel-ground to form a concave surface, rather than a flat plane.

Hone   A fine-grained abrasive stone, or the process of giving a keen edge to a cutting tool.

Joint   The sharpening process of making all teeth of a saw or all edges of a cutterhead the same, exact height in its line of cut or its cutting circle, so that each one does its equal share of cutting.

Kerf The cutting path made by a saw.

Lap Using a hand surface with abrasive granules to smooth or polish another surface so that it is perfectly flat.

Lip Name given to the cutting edges on drills and boring tools.

Nick Damage to a tool's edge (like a dent or notch) made by striking a hard object.

Pitch Resinous secretions from wood that adhere to cutting tools.

Quench To cool hot metal in water or a special liquid bath.

Rake (See *cutting angle*).

Rolled Edge An edge formed by burnishing such as the edge of a scraper.

Secondary Bevel (also called *micro bevel*). A bevel formed just behind the cutting edge to support and strengthen it by increasing the degree of the ground bevel.

Set The outward bending of steel saw teeth that results in the cutting of a saw kerf that is wider than the thickness of the blade.

Shank The part of a rotary bit or tool held by the collet or chuck.

Slick A home-made sharpening tool that consists of sheet abrasive on a piece of flat wood.

Slipstone A small, hand-held abrasive stone of various cross-sectional shapes used to hone cutting edges.

Slurry A watery, mud-like mixture.

Spiral Cutters Special, difficult-to-sharpen tools that have helical or coil-like cutting edges and flutes, as opposed to straight ones.

Spur A sharp point or edge of a rotary bit or tool designed to sever cross-grain wood fibres.

Strop To make a keen edge by stroking away from the cutting edge with leather or a composition material.

Temper The correct heat treatment of a tool's metal, used to make it sharp.

Tool Rest Part of a machine on which a tool is supported or held.

Tripoli A fine-abrasive polishing compound.

Veining Tool (also known as a parting tool). A V-shaped gouge.

Vortex An air-flow, whirlpool action rotating about an axis.

Whet The process of rubbing on or with an abrasive stone to sharpen an edge. Also known as honing.

Whetstone A fine-grit abrasive used to wear away metal to create a finer edge than that produced from grinding with coarse abrasives.

Wire Edge See burr.

Index